THE
STRENGTH
OF OUR DREAMS

ALSO BY SARA HENDERSON

From Strength to Strength
The Strength in Us All
From Strength to Strength (audio tape)
Some of My Friends Have Tails
Outback Wisdom
A Year at Bullo

SARA HENDERSON

THE
STRENGTH
OF OUR DREAMS

SUN
Pan Macmillan Australia

First published 1998 in Macmillan by Pan Macmillan Australia Pty Limited
First published 1999 in Sun by Pan Macmillan Australia Pty Limited
St Martins Tower, 31 Market Street, Sydney

National Library of Australia
cataloguing-in-publication data:

Henderson, Sara, 1936– .

The strength of our dreams.

ISBN 0 7251 0763 4.

1. Henderson, Sara, 1936– . 2. Businesswomen – Northern
Territory – Darwin Interviews. 3. Women ranchers – Northern Territory
– Bullo River Station – Biography. 4. Bullo River Station (N.T.). I. Title.

636.0092

Typeset in 12.9/15.5 Bembo by Midland Typesetters
Printed in Australia by McPherson's Printing Group

To guardian angels . . . and Charlie

It's time.
Time to open the door to my heart
and let in the angel of love.
Time to love again.
Time to think about things
yet to be done.
Time to dream dreams
yet to be won.
In my heart I know . . .
the best is yet to come!

CONTENTS

ACKNOWLEDGEMENTS

As life continues to be a charmed existence, I realise more and more each day it depends on so many, many people for it to stay that way.

'you never really achieve anything in life on your own'

If you analyse any of your achievements you will find someone has helped you somewhere along the way.

So many people have helped me with my writing career. My publisher, the sales reps, my publicists, the designers, editors, booksellers and most important of all, you, the reader.

I thank you all and a special thanks this time goes to Cath—she knows why.

PREFACE

Ever since *The Strength in Us All* was published in 1994, I have been receiving letters and phone calls, basically asking, 'What's happening now?' So I was very tempted to name this book just that, as it answers the much-asked questions and brings you up to date on the Bullo saga!

But *The Strength of Our Dreams* (the third book in the Strength Series) is a much better title, because it describes the book perfectly. This book finally brings Charlie's dream to reality, and along the way, as we struggled to achieve Charlie's dream, we have developed the strength to turn quite a few of our dreams into reality.

However, even when dreams are coming true, life keeps throwing curved balls at you. I hope as you read how we've dealt with our problems over the past five and a half years, you gain strength and ideas to apply to your own life. For, as one man said after reading *From Strength to Strength*, 'If a bloody sheila can do it, so can I!' And what's more, he did, saving his business and going on to further success.

We have been through the lot—emotional worries, financial strains, physical danger and high drama—I know all these facets of life will continue as long as life itself. But if you look at the other side of life's ledger—health, family, love, happiness, freedom and achievement—these far outweigh the problems and difficulties every time. Keeping the right attitude towards life, by focusing on the positive side of the ledger, can make your journey one long interesting, exciting road, with each and every day full of new challenges.

Life is there for the taking, all you have to do is take it. Once you have it in your hand you are in control, where there is no limit to your achievements. Reach for the heavens and God just might hand you an armful of stars.

CHAPTER 1

October 1993–
November 1993

A ringing phone shattered a very deep sleep. Through bleary eyes I could see it was 5.30 a.m. and was about to ask the hotel's operator if he knew what time it was when I heard Franz's voice. I was awake instantly, all my instincts telling me something was wrong. I was right. They had been mustering Nutwood Paddock and Marlee's horse had slipped in mud on the edge of the billabong at full gallop.

The horse came down heavily, Marlee's head and shoulder taking the brunt of the fall. Franz and Gordon Boag, our Kiwi stockman, were the only other people on the property. Franz hadn't been part of a medical emergency evacuation before, but with Marlee unconscious he had no choice so he went ahead. At first, he was told by the Northern Territory Health Service to drive Marlee to Katherine, but he refused, saying she could have head and spinal injuries and so he wanted a plane. Franz is very definite in his requests and he got his plane. The accident had happened right on sunset the previous night so the earliest plane into the station would be at first light.

I held my breath through the explanation waiting to hear how Marlee was. Franz finally reached this part of the report. He thought that her shoulder might be broken and was worried about her having a fractured skull. Marlee had been in and out of consciousness all night, not making any sense at all. Every time Franz asked her a question about Air Medical, she talked about the mustering. She knew her name and where she was, but was confused about what had happened and kept harping on this. I said I would fly straight home and meet Marlee at the hospital in Darwin.

My ailing brain snapped into action and I threw my clothes into the suitcase, called the airport and got a seat on the jet to Darwin leaving Sydney at 7 a.m. I raced down to the foyer to check out only to find about one hundred Japanese tourists checking in, so didn't bother and left a note for the concierge.

I was in Sydney recording an abridged version of *From Strength to Strength* on cassette. When my publishers had first asked me if I could do this, I told them I had no idea. I had been hopeless in school plays and thought I would probably mess this up too.

They pointed out how popular my book tours were and how the audience loved to listen to my stories. I wasn't convinced. I didn't think I could ramble along on tape as I did when telling my stories to an audience, but didn't voice this concern. We would soon find out if I was any good.

When I arrived at my publisher's office for the first recording session I voiced my doubts about my ability to carry this off. I was assured there was no pressure on me—if I was no good, no problem, they would hire a professional to do the job. So it was off to the sound recording studio to see.

I arrived at the studio with my editor, Julia, and we met Peter, who was in charge of recording. I was happy to learn a few minutes reading was all that was necessary for him to know if I had the right voice and timing for recording. I was sure the whole thing would be over in a few minutes. Not so. Unfortunately for me Peter thought I was a natural and that I could give the reading the emotion that no-one else could. I was told a few tricks of the trade, given some coaching, and was plunged into yet another new world. One which required me to live on my nerves and perform once more.

The recording equipment was so sensitive that it picked up a page turning or if I moved my feet and a deep breath sounded like a clap of thunder. So I had to sit stock still with my breathing regular and shallow. I could only breathe deeply at the end of a page where it could be edited out and could only turn a page at a full stop for the same reason. With all this in the back of my mind, I then had to sound relaxed and full of expression!

October 1993–November 1993

The session went well and being exhausted actually helped with the recording—I had no energy to be nervous, and the tiredness gave my voice a quality of calmness, and kept the breathing regular and shallow. We were now almost one third of the way along the two-hour recording with two sessions to go.

This second recording session, six weeks after the first, provided crucial evidence that my hectic schedule was taking its toll and I needed to slow down. One disturbing problem was that unbeknown to me, I was reading words and whole sentences that simply weren't on the page in front of me. After I was asked to read one particular paragraph for the third time, I asked in frustration, 'Just how do you want me to read this, I have done it every way I can! I'm sorry, you will have to show me what you want.'

'Nothing wrong with the reading. I just want you to read the words that are there,' Peter replied.

I carefully re-read the paragraph.

'You did it again,' said Peter.

I could not for the world see what he was talking about, and frustrated said I had read what was on the page in front of me. Peter replayed the tape, and to my amazement my version was totally off the planet. I had added and changed words making the meaning of the paragraph completely different and nothing to do with the surrounding story. I underlined the words I had changed and it was many takes before I could get through the reading with it sounding OK.

4

I was up to the sad part of the book where Charlie, Mum and Marlee's Charlie die. In the condensed version they all pile in on each other and I just couldn't get through one sentence without crying. It was dreadful. The session just went on and on, with me crying and apologising. Sometimes just looking at the script was enough to set me off. We kept taking breaks and I would walk around the building, sobbing uncontrollably. After a good cry I'd think I was in control, only to pick up the script and burst into tears again, without uttering a word! It got to the point where I could only record a few sentences at a time without my voice breaking. Peter decided to record with the emotional breaks in my voice. Firstly, it was genuine emotion and secondly, I think he knew he wasn't going to get this part any other way. So I cried, stopped, walked and stumbled through until we reached a lighter part. But there was still so much sadness in my voice we cut the session short, hoping I would be better the next day. Although the following morning was when I heard of Marlee's accident and I didn't show up.

When I reached Sydney airport I called Franz, who told me Marlee was being airlifted to Katherine Hospital. I was horrified. Why wasn't she going to Darwin Hospital? Katherine didn't have anywhere near the facilities of Darwin and with suspected head and spinal injuries, Marlee should have been taken to Darwin. I was fuming! Stupid policy had come into the equation— Bullo is in the so-called Katherine district so off they toddled to Katherine!

To get to Marlee in Katherine from Darwin that day I would have to hire a private aircraft. I certainly wasn't going to face the hours of driving on the highway, but in retrospect maybe I should have! The only plane I could get on such short notice was a trainer plane owned by a friend. The necessity of having our own plane on the station was very clear at this point of my frantic arrangements. But I had to remind myself that Marlee was the only pilot on the station at the moment.

Franz was about to solo, but that was a few weeks away. Not that that would have stopped him getting Marlee to hospital if a plane had been there.

I arrived in Darwin around 1 p.m. When I got to the Aero club and saw the plane I almost cried. It was about the size of a pocket handkerchief, and comfort was not a word one would associate with it. I was hot, exhausted, and worried sick about Marlee and was about to be squashed into a flying peapod for the journey to Katherine.

I arrived in Katherine hours later, a wreck. The flight had taken forever! The plane had a glass dome roof, so I had fried in the midday sun and perspiration ran down my stockinged legs, making my shoes soggy. My claustrophobia had surfaced during the flight with a vengeance and I spent most of the trip with my eyes closed. The pilot must have thought I was mad, answering questions with my head down and eyes closed and fanning myself.

The weather was not on our side either. With storms everywhere the young keen pilot at the controls was sashaying all over the sky, and when we weren't doing that, turbulence was throwing the plane about. I was on the verge of throwing up when we touched down, so as we taxied up to the terminal I opened the door and hung my head out to get some fresh air.

Once inside the terminal I staggered into the bathroom and poured water over my head. I didn't care what happened to my hair or my suit, I just had to get cool. A vision of disaster looked back at me from the mirror—wet, wind blown and knotted hair plastered down on a haggard face which showed definite signs of sleep deprivation, worry lines, and a recent addition, severe sunburn. I didn't give a stuff, and just walked out to the horn-blowing taxi the pilot had kindly called for me.

At 5.30 p.m. after travelling for 12 hours, I walked into the hospital. I was about to ask the woman at the reception desk where I could find Marlee, when she took one look at me and said, 'Emergency is the next door down.'

Marlee was asleep, and seemed OK. I sagged thankfully onto the chair and waited. Eventually she opened her eyes and greeted me with a grin that told me she wasn't really with it. She smiled sweetly and said, 'Hi Mum,' then closed her eyes again.

There was no-one I could find who could give me any information, but I was told the doctor would be there soon. So I took Marlee's hand, pulled the chair close to her bed, and put my head down and slept.

The next thing I knew it was nine o'clock and a nurse was shaking my shoulder. It seemed I had slept through the doctor's visit—the nurse said he had taken one look at me and said not to wake me as I looked like I could do with the rest. So I was still none the wiser as to Marlee's condition. I was so disorientated and in such a state the nurse took pity on me and brought me a cup of tea and several biscuits—the first food for the whole day. I composed myself to a degree and called a cab. I kissed my sleeping Marlee goodnight, she momentarily opened her eyes, smiled again, said, 'Hi Mum,' and went back to sleep.

As soon as I arrived at the motel I called Franz. He had talked to the doctor and had more information than me, even though he was in the middle of nowhere and I'd been in the hospital all afternoon. From the examinations done the doctor didn't think Marlee had a fractured skull, and was sure it was only concussion. And although her shoulder wasn't good, there was so much bruising and swelling he couldn't tell if the bone was broken or not. The doctor had ordered X-rays of both her head and shoulder and would have the results tomorrow. I put down the phone and sat under a cold shower then crawled over to the bed still wet and went to sleep.

I had planned to be at the hospital early the next day, but slept through to nine and still felt dreadful. I called my publishers and apologised for not turning up for the recording session, and all was forgiven when they heard about Marlee.

My hair was a major problem—I couldn't get a comb through it. But after a few washes and a lot of conditioner, it finally looked presentable. My face was still glowing bright red from sunburn, but a heavy layer of face powder toned it down a fraction. I had no other clothes than the ones I had dropped on the floor the previous night, so I ironed the blouse and skirt, and left the wrinkled jacket in the wardrobe. But I needed more clothes, as heaven knew how long I was going to be in Katherine.

I found a clothing store a few blocks away and bought some cotton shorts, T-shirts, a pair of sandals and a straw hat. I changed into one of the outfits in the change room, put on the hat and my sunglasses and caught a cab to the hospital. I looked a little more normal, but still felt like hell.

The day was spent with me holding Marlee's hand and sleeping with my head resting on her bed. Marlee would wake periodically, say, 'Hi Mum,' still smiling that 'off in the wild blue yonder' smile and drift off again. I missed the doctor again on his morning rounds. He was getting a bit concerned about me by now, but didn't wake me, just left a message.

We finally met around four o'clock. It was good news. The X-rays showed no fracture of the skull, just severe concussion. The shoulder had no breaks, but was severely injured. It would have been better for the healing process if the bone had broken as there was such extensive bruising and swelling it would take forever to heal. The doctor recommended to start physio on the shoulder as soon as possible while the concussion needed rest. The two instructions for cure seeming in conflict in my mind.

The next day at the hospital Marlee was awake more than me but I was still not getting much more than 'Hi

Mum' and the wild grin out of her. But I could see there was intense thinking going on behind those beautiful eyes. They darted constantly around the room, taking everything in and trying to work out just what was happening and why she was there. She reminded me of a wild animal that's found itself in strange surroundings and is not quite sure how to escape.

After four days of virtually continuous sleep at the hospital and at the motel, I started to feel slightly alive. Although at the beginning, the more I slept, the worse I felt. Yet I knew I needed the rest. I suppose my body was slowly relaxing, unwinding from the uptight spring I had wound myself into over the years, and in the unravelling there were bound to be side effects. Feeling bloody awful seemed to be one of them.

Marlee on the other hand was recovering at a much faster pace. I kept waking to find her watching me, and our conversation finally got past the 'Hi Mum' stage. Apart from a terrible headache, her shoulder was the worst of her injuries, and years later it is still giving her trouble. The concussion gave her temporary memory loss and she still remembers nothing after the horse went down. One minute she was galloping along, mustering cattle, the next thing she knew she was in the house, lying on the bed, with Franz and Gordon peering anxiously at her.

As Franz was a few weeks off his solo licence, to get Marlee home from hospital, Ron Lawford, Franz's instructor, flew down to Bullo and Franz flew the plane into Katherine. It was still early morning when they arrived as Franz and Ron had left the station at very first light, so we took off before the cool air gave away to the heat of the day.

To ensure a smooth flight with no violent lurches into air pockets for our patient, Franz flew high at eight-thousand feet. When you are flying above the earth amongst massive clouds that tower twenty thousand feet into the air, the feeling is one of awe and privilege at being so close to such massive towers of power, and in some cases destruction. The clouds this morning, however, were friendly, and no 'Charlie Bravos' (storm and thunder clouds) were in sight. Just white and silver iridescent balls of cotton wool that looked all the world like they had light bulbs inside them. I do a lot of my best creative thinking when cloud flying and as we only get such cloud formations during the wet—which is the time I write—it fits in nicely.

Today, however, my thoughts were mainly on Marlee. I was still very worried about her as the Marlee I knew was still not in evidence. I had a smiling Marlee who wasn't quite sure of what had happened, but the doctor said this was normal. It could take up to ten days of rest before she'd start to be her old self, and another week in bed before she was really on the mend. So I decided to watch her closely, and if I wasn't satisfied with her progress, we would fly to Darwin for further tests.

I stared out the window at the clouds and thought some more sober thoughts, this time about myself. I couldn't remember when I had slept four days straight. The year had been filled with wall-to-wall appointments all around Australia. My problems stemmed from being

11

in popular demand and as I was new to the world of celebrity, I hadn't learned to say 'No'. My daily mantra had simply become 'Just get through to December'. My body had been giving me warning signals and my doctor told me to slow down but he knew that none of the Bullo women knew how to stop working.

I had the distinct feeling I had just been saved from something dreadful. Every part of me was aching, but I was very conscious that something major was happening in my body.

Had I just stepped back from plunging over a precipice? All my instincts answered a sober 'Yes'. If so, why had I been saved? And more mysteriously, what had saved me? I looked over at Marlee asleep with that dreamy smile still lighting up her face, and decided I really do have a guardian angel.

In this major turning point of my life, I was saved by my Marlee. If her horse hadn't fallen, I would have surely had a breakdown of some kind, fallen over the edge of the cliff into that black hole of nothingness people descend into when they have nervous breakdowns. I took Marlee's hand to thank her silently. Without opening her eyes, her lips shaped, 'Hi Mum,' and she smiled.

When I looked out the window again I could see the welcoming cliffs of Bullo River looking back at me, waiting patiently.

When we got home if I wasn't sleeping, I would drag myself around to do the bare minimum. I asked Franz to tell all the people calling the station I was away for weeks which took care of hours of phone calls while I slowly regained my mental and physical health.

Everyone was counting the days to our housekeeper Jacqui's return, especially the men. But Jacqui wasn't due back until the 12th December, Marlee was out of action for a few more weeks, so all they had was me.

Jacqui was at Heytesbury Stud—where she worked before coming to Bullo—for two months to help with the foaling. When she was first asked to do this at the beginning of September her reply was no, as she had a job at Bullo and was too busy. But as the month progressed, Marlee and I could see she was worried about the mares and their foals.

As the calls increased with discussions about a particular mare, or problems with another pregnancy, we could see we had to let her go and care for the horses that needed her. It was devastating for us, but we knew how much we loved our animals and without a doubt Jacqui loved the mares she had left back at Heytesbury, just outside of Perth, as if they were her own.

Marlee was doing all the exercises the physio at the hospital had given her, but the shoulder was getting worse. So Franz took her off to Darwin to see our doctor.

I continued to hibernate, sleeping day and night, only surfacing to cook a meal now and again for poor Gordon. The night Marlee and Franz arrived back, I really got my act together and baked a leg of lamb with all the trimmings, and Gordon who'd been eating steak and chips every meal was in seventh heaven. But as much as you never get tired of compliments about your cooking, I was counting the days until Jacqui returned, so I could get out of the kitchen.

I only had one more week at home then it was off to Sydney again for a conference, and to finish the book recording. The phone had been running hot with requests for me to go places. And as hard as it was for me to refuse, as some of the requests were for really worthy causes, I steeled myself and learned to say 'No' without feeling guilty. Whenever I started to weaken, I would remember the jibbering mess I was back in October and then could say 'No' quite easily.

I received a call from my booking agent asking me to do a conference on the 25th November and I said 'No'.

'But you have two free days before you go home,' came the reply.

'No I don't,' I replied quietly.

'Yes you do, I have your schedule here in front of me and you have the 25th and the 26th free.'

'What you have in front of you on the computer is my working schedule. I do not have the 25th and the 26th free.' I waited. I was still a long way from being well and those two days were for resting. But being young she thought otherwise.

'Ahhh, I see,' came the knowing reply. 'Well, have a great time! I'll tell the people you are not available . . . for speaking!' She assumed I was having a romantic weekend, well I could have rallied energy for that! Unfortunately it would just be an uninteresting rest period, but I didn't bother explaining this.

—·—

I arrived in Sydney late in the afternoon, spoke at the conference at lunchtime the following day and had dinner with my publisher. I could feel a change in myself, not a major one, but I was definitely more on the ball with what was happening around me, not vague and just smiling. But the big test would be the recording session the following day.

It was just over four weeks since recording the last session with all the breaking down and walking around the building. The change in me in that short period of time was amazing. I had a few emotional parts, but on the whole the session went very well—much to my relief and, I am sure, of everyone else present. It was such a success we rerecorded some of the second taping and the very beginning where my voice sounded too formal and nervous.

I left for home on the 28 November, having refused many Christmas parties, speeches for school break-ups and fund-raising functions. I had to take care of myself and that would take months, not weeks. Although December was going to be fairly busy, I didn't have to travel anywhere for the whole month! But only because I had said that little word 'No' about twenty times in the last few weeks of November.

CHAPTER 2

December 1993–
January 1994

*I*t was December and hot. Storms with amazing cloud
formations were the order of the day. December and
January are also the rainbow and butterfly months on
Bullo River.

Mostly at sunrise and sunset beautiful rainbows form
in the north-east corner of the valley. And butterflies
float through the house, resting on a chair, on a picture
frame, on the top of a tomato sauce bottle.

However there are drawbacks to wet season. This is
the time we get bugs by the thousands, mosquitoes by
the millions and just about every other thing that flies
or crawls. But this year despite the heat, the bugs, the
mosquitoes, it was bliss because I didn't have to travel
for a month.

I settled down to writing and sharing the cooking
with Marlee who was back to her bright and cheerful
self—it was now only twelve days till Jacqui would be

16

back! We were counting the days until we could hand the house back to her, and were very busy cleaning as the house certainly had not had the loving care Jacqui gave it. Despite all this work, when Jacqui returned she soon had it up to 'J' standard and regular meals became the norm again, making Franz very happy.

Marlee's shoulder was still giving her lots of pain, but we both knew the recovery period would be a long haul. The doctor had told Marlee this, and we both remembered when I had a similar injury years before, and many times Marlee had to lift a roast into the oven for me, because my shoulder just wouldn't work. The tissue damage in my shoulder never really healed and this is very evident when I have a massage and that shoulder has more clicks and clacks than my whole body put together.

We were heading into a busy Christmas, with Danielle and Martin arriving on the 23rd and an Austrian invasion—Herman, Gepherdt and Gunther, three of Franz's friends, were coming to experience an Outback Christmas.

Sometime during the first three weeks of December Marlee and I made the yearly road trek to Darwin to do the Christmas shopping. The station wagon and the poor old one-tonne trailer were loaded down to the springs and it was a very slow trip home. With a house full of family and friends and staff helping with the hay planting, we had quite a load of food and presents to haul back from town.

I did many Christmas radio interviews throughout three states. I was asked about the weather, what work

17

we did at this time of the year, did we celebrate Christmas Day the same as people down south. It was strange to be asked these questions; it felt as if we were living on the moon. But I suppose if they had read about my first Christmas on Bullo with the stuffed grey, boiled ox heart on a tin plate, people might think we *are* a different race.

All the interviews got around to asking me to say words of encouragement to people on the land and to people in general. In December 1993 there wasn't much hope or enthusiasm around, as the country didn't seem to be going anywhere. So I did my best to ignite the Christmas spirit. I was well on the road to rest and recovery and so had good reason to feel optimistic. I had family, love, friends, a beautiful home, rain and feed for the animals—almost everything a person could wish for. But I was acutely aware that lots of people had nothing and faced a bleak Christmas knowing no cheer. So my Christmas wish was for these people.

I did have one reason to feel sorry for myself during December. It was time to pay Trippe's legal fees following the judgement handed down by the appeal court. In 1986, only weeks after my Charlie had died, his cousin, Gus Trippe, sued me for half a million dollars for late delivery of cattle. This was in accordance with a deal signed by him and Charlie—a settlement of all their business dealings over decades. How unfair this ruling was I won't go into, and years later I still smoulder over this. But I am not alone, so many people have shared with me their miserable encounters with our legal system. As one lawyer had the blatant audacity to say to me when I asked him the question, 'Do you call that fair, do you call that justice?': 'You do not go to court for justice you go to court for the financial settlement of a dispute.'

I accepted the inevitable and parted with our hard-earned cash to pay legal fees. I had already paid out the amount the court handed down in the judgement—not half a million, thank heavens, but just over a quarter of a million dollars. Now it was time to pay his legal fees, along with my own, which eventually brought the amount back to half a million dollars! Then another disaster struck: Marlee's beloved dog Hunter was diagnosed with cancer. After such a lovely Christmas, these two events made it a very sad farewell to 1993 indeed.

As sad as I was at losing Hunter, Marlee was devastated. He was a wonderful dog and her soulmate for so long. Franz had taken him to town to the vet because he had a bad tooth, but it turned out to be cancer of the jaw. On a very sad phone call, Marlee and I cried as she agreed it would be best to have him put to sleep at the surgery. Franz was very thoughtful and brought him home in the plane and buried him in our cemetery here on Bullo along with my Jedda and all our other animals.

Looking at my 1994 diary had my thoughts immediately turning to my health and my continued desire to keep on the road to recovery. Already I had too many conference bookings, along with book tours for Australia and New Zealand, and all the publicity that goes with the launch of a new book. So in January I would start saying 'No' to any other engagements for 1994.

I read somewhere it takes a supertanker eight miles to turn around or to come to a halt in the water, such is its weight and forward motion once it gets going. Well I equate trying to get my life under control to a super-tanker trying to turn around or stop—it is a mammoth job! It ended up taking all of three years before I achieved this objective to a healthy satisfaction. The most important thing I learned was to watch the engagements booked for twelve and eighteen months ahead.

It is sometimes hard for people to understand why I am not available eighteen months down the track. But after I patiently explain a few of my commitments, they are usually very sympathetic.

And then they promptly ask if they can book me two and a half years ahead!

As sad as the end of 1993 was, we were looking forward to a better year in 1994. Although the sadness of losing Hunter lingered for Marlee, we did have a lively New Year's Eve with friends and some of the staff staying on over the wet season to help with the hay planting.

New Year's Day was very hot, so there was very little movement around the homestead with animals and people seeking out the coolest spot—usually the same place. So man and beast could be found scattered at regular intervals around the homestead, both snoring soundly through the heat of the day.

The 2nd was Danielle's birthday, and she and Martin were finally on their way to New Zealand for their honeymoon. They were married in Darwin in September on

Charlie's birthday. It was a wonderful event despite a certain amount of tension in the air. My daughter Bonnie and her husband Arthur had recently published very nasty articles in a gossip weekly and made some very heartbreaking statements. After Charlie died Bonnie sued me for what she claimed were wages due. I could handle the monetary aspect of this, but when she testified in court against me I found it hard to forgive her. These two heartbreaking events were followed by petty articles in the gossip magazines so they were not my favourite couple.

Fraser, one of Charlie's sons living in America, came over to give Danielle away. I had not heard from him since 1986 when, after his father's death, he called from America to ask me if I had a new will Charlie had written which disinherited me and left everything to him and the rest of the children. When I asked him if indeed Charlie had written this new will, did he really think Charlie would give it to me, the stupidity of his question finally dawned on him. Besides, I informed him, Charlie had no assets in his name, except the sailing boat. Everything else was in the company's name and that had belonged to me since 1964.

He then said he would like a share of the money from the sale of the boat. I told him gladly, if he also took a share of the debts his father left. He wasn't interested in honouring his father's debts, but he did have a Sydney lawyer contact Charlie's lawyer and ask about this new will. He was told the only will on hand was the one Charlie had signed in their office and they knew of no other. The lawyer requested a copy of the will and was told, as Fraser was not part of the will, he would not be able to see a copy unless the trustee gave permission. As I was the trustee of the estate, he knew he wouldn't have much luck going down that road. So as you can imagine, our greeting at the wedding was extremely formal.

So there we all were, together to celebrate Danielle and Martin's wedding smiling and being polite. I don't think I would have gone through all that stress for anyone but Danielle. I was determined not to do anything to spoil her wedding day. I think everyone tried very hard, but each day presented difficult situations to overcome. We made it through a dreadfully strained family dinner the night before the wedding and I know Danielle was worried someone might explode. After we'd made it through the dinner without telling each other exactly what we thought, I am sure she worried her whole wedding day that the explosion might still come. But, I am happy to say, the wedding went smoothly and it was a very successful day.

Franz and Marlee usually handled the hay planting, but after increasing the acreage in recent years it had become quite a job. It was too difficult to complete all the ploughing and planting in the short time available before the rains made the ground too wet to work. So we were lucky this year that some of our budding stockmen were also very good farmers, and had decided to stay on. This meant both Marlee and Franz had a rest from the midnight 'red-eye' tractor driving shift.

The help was also valuable for another reason. Our

farming equipment, well-used and second-hand when we bought it in the eighties, was now showing definite signs of wear. Franz spent about as much time in the workshop patching and replacing parts as he did ploughing, so to have extra help made his job so much easier. He repaired breakdowns while the men kept the farming moving along at a regular pace. We knew that next year new machinery would have to be part of the budget.

The days were filled with ploughing, planting and the major pastime, scaring the cockatoos away from the paddocks. They had to be stopped from digging up the seeds the first ten days or so after planting, then again after the young seedlings poked their heads through the soil. If not kept at bay, the cockatoos walk along the rows of new plants, pull them out, then drop them on the ground, not even bothering to eat them, just leaving them to die. It is destruction in its purest form. If left to their own devices, they can destroy a whole crop as they descend onto a field in the thousands at first light of daybreak, every day!

My health was improving daily as I slept, worked and exercised. It was such a treat to be in tune with the world around me again, not standing back and watching everything in the detached manner I had been. Not travelling for a whole month had been such good medicine, causing such a feeling of excitement each day when I woke.

At the beginning of January Franz and the 'A team'— the name I had given Herman, Gepherdt and

23

Gunther—were busy packing for a fishing and overnight camping trip down on the Victoria River, near the mouth of the Bullo. Our A team returned with their first barra, or the only one they didn't eat, and their first Australian sunburn. After only one day on the river they looked like they had been roughing it for at least a few weeks. They all seemed very pleased to be back from the wilderness—even though they had been only twelve miles away from the homestead the entire time.

The next day I received a surprise phone call from Frances Mason, a friend I met when we lived in Maryland back in the sixties and her husband Jack who was an old sailing buddy of Charlie's. Frances's lovely American accent travelled across the thousands of miles and came loud and clear into the homestead in outback Australia.

She had read in the English magazine, *Hello*, that the Duchess of York had been given a book by her sister called *From Strength to Strength*, written by an Australian author, Sara Henderson. She wondered if it was me, and was calling to find out. She was quite excited when I told her yes, and she said a friend of hers in Alice Springs was sending the book to her. Her friend had read the book and told Frances she would also enjoy it. Over the years Frances has sent Christmas cards every year, but I have been very remiss, only managing about one every five years or so. So I was fairly up to date with what was happening in her life and when the book arrived she was about to catch up on mine.

This call was one of the many which came from

friends in America who had received my book from people living in Australia. The book was also about to go to Austria. Herman was staying on Bullo for a few more months, but Gepherdt and Gunther were off home, and my book was going with them. They had a wonderful visit and we enjoyed having them. Franz had a wonderful time with them in the workshop, each one helping him with their particular skill.

We were now down to one dog, Franz's Mr Mustang— a very playful half-grown puppy, who was so devoted to his master he didn't want to spend time with anyone else. On our way back from Christmas shopping in Darwin Marlee had arranged to get a Rottweiler puppy for me for Christmas. The litter was only just born and too young to leave their mother, so she made arrangements for my puppy to come out to Bullo on the mail plane. The puppy arrived in the first week of January, still so tiny she could sit comfortably in my hand. I was overjoyed to have another puppy.

I, of course, was writing, so I put Sumie in a basket on the floor next to my chair, and there she stayed. She was the quietest puppy I had ever had, but I thought this was good considering I sit most of the day in the office writing or doing office work.

But there was something wrong. She was eating, drinking milk and the colour of her mouth and eyes was good, but she was covered with tiny ticks. I spent a whole day taking off as many as I could, but with her thick, fluffy hair it was impossible to clean her properly

25

and I couldn't dip her as she was too young. I called Sarah, our vet, and she said it was probably the ticks which were making her listless and quiet. She said for Marlee to give an injection of a minute dose of Ivamec which would kill the ticks, and I would just have to watch her from there. If she was eating and starting to take interest in things around her, we didn't have to worry. If there was no improvement, we should call back. Sumie perked up a little the next day after her injection, but the following morning was not the least bit interested in food or play. There was something very wrong: this puppy wasn't quiet by nature, she was sick. Luckily, we had hired an aircraft for a few months so Franz was able to fly Sumie straight to Kununurra.

A low-pressure area moved in over the valley later that afternoon, and we had bad weather for days. So she was one very lucky puppy in many ways—if Franz hadn't gone that morning, the weather would have prevented him from flying for days.

Sarah rang to say Sumie had so many worms in her system they were eating through the walls of the blood vessels. She had been sick when she arrived at Bullo, but I mistook it for a quiet nature. The pilot of the mail plane had remarked when he arrived with her how good and how well behaved she was for a puppy. He had taken her out of her box and she lay completely still on the seat next to him for the entire flight. We now know why!

Coming from a breeder, I just assumed she had been wormed and Marlee was told she was current with all her injections. So I wasn't even thinking of worm medicine for at least a few more weeks! Sarah said the injection

Marlee gave Sumie to get rid of the ticks actually saved her life, because it also killed the worms inside her little body. The trouble was she was also bleeding internally and was not winning this battle. Franz got her there in the nick of time but as it was, the diagnosis was not good. All that could be done for the puppy was being done, but Sarah warned me, 'Be prepared, she might not come home.'

We had not been having a good run with our dogs. As I waited anxiously, Sarah was very patient and sweet, updating me with regular reports. Sumie made it through the first two days after a blood transfusion, but I was not to get my hopes up just yet, I was told, as it was a long way to go before we could consider the puppy safe and on the way to recovery.

Sumie's tiny, empty basket sat forlornly in the corner, catching my eye and reminding me of the sweet little black ball of fluff that for just a short time had been part of my life. I moved the basket out of sight and tried to put little Sumie out of my thoughts.

The low-pressure area moved away and the sun came out. Sarah called the same day to say Sumie was off the critical list but she wanted to keep her for a few more days until she recovered a little more strength. Sarah had been taking Sumie home with her each night and the puppy was becoming quite playful. This was a Sumie I was yet to see! I was grateful to Sarah who through her care and love was responsible for Sumie making a full recovery. After such good news I moved Sumie's basket back into my office and placed it on the floor next to my desk and waited for her return.

After all of nine days in hospital, a healthy and very playful puppy arrived back in the plane with Franz. I had to keep her away from Mr Mustang for a while, as he was six months older and far too rough for this small ten-week-old recovery patient. So Sumie spent her days in my office playing with toys in her basket, while I wrote.

With the holidays over, the phone was back to ringing every half an hour. I was going to need an operator soon at this rate! I had one call from quite a character who said he was starting up a cattle empire. I patiently listened to all his plans for the next twenty years. After this enthusiastic rundown, he finally got around to the reason for the call. He was interested in breeding bulls, and could we help. The way he was talking I visualised a sale of a few hundred to stock his great cattle empire and said we might be able to supply some of his needs. Just how many bulls did he have in mind, I asked.

'One,' came the proud reply.

'One!' I exclaimed, amazed.

'Well, there could be a further purchase later on,' mumbled the big spender.

I told him the price and said yes, we could fill his whole order without much delay. My sarcasm fell on deaf ears, as he was busy accepting the deal with such attention to detail, you would think we were moving ten thousand bulls! The next question really floored me.

'Do you deliver?'

I collected myself sufficiently to reply, 'Only if you purchase one hundred and fifty!'

28

We didn't deliver, no-one delivered, but this fellow had a lot to learn, and I knew hell would freeze over before he ever purchased one hundred and fifty bulls. So I was safe with my free freight offer.

The no delivery seemed to put a spoke in his massive livestock purchase plan. But he was not at a loss for solutions. 'If I bring my utility over there, could I tie him on a lead in the back?' A semi-wild, young, eight hundred kilo bull was not something you put in an open Toyota on a lead! These cattle would have to be fully enclosed in strong crates to travel, but our new cattle king thought the animal would stand still during a seven-hour journey in the back of a Toyota!

It took me a lot longer this time to gather myself and in between lots of coughing to cover my laughter, I managed to get out, 'No, I don't think so.'

'Pity,' came the thoughtful reply.

I could see endless wasted time moving this one bull, so I told him I would arrange for the bull to go to Katherine with the next load of cattle leaving the station. How the cattle baron got him from the Katherine stockyards to his vast spread of a hundred acres, I never found out. But I often wonder if he tried to tie the bull on a lead in the back of his utility.

I almost didn't answer the next call, worried it would be the cattle king again with some indepth question about his great venture into the livestock market. Luckily I did; it was our lawyer. BTEC had dropped the case against us for moving untested cattle off the property. The previous July, we had received news that the BTEC (the Brucellosis, Tuberculosis Eradication

29

Campaign) sued Marlee for moving untested cattle off the property. But charge Marlee and you were charging me or vice versa. So we braced ourselved to face yet another court case. Again we were in the right, but we were bitterly aware this meant nothing in the so-called courts of justice. The case was over a silly paperwork mistake, but no-one on their side would admit to the mistake.

It seems the only justice you get these days is when you don't go to court and I was very happy with the news. The relief of not having to go to court took a great weight off my mind and I went on writing with renewed enthusiasm.

One of the very first calls of the next day gave me the news that Noel Buntine had died. Another legend of the north gone. I will always remember when Noel and Charlie first met. Charlie, dressed in moleskins and shiny riding boots, was waiting impatiently, wondering why there was a delay loading the cattle. He walked over to a fellow working under the truck. Charlie, in his inimitable and infuriating way, said jokingly, 'You don't think I am going to put my cattle in that broken down heap, do you?'

'You don't think I am going to load those *&#$@@* cattle into my good truck, do you?' came the instant reply.

Charlie took offence immediately, suddenly losing his sense of humour. 'You're a bit of a cheeky bugger, aren't you!'

'Yeh, you might say that,' came the disinterested reply.

'Well, I just might report you to your boss. How does that affect you?'

'Not much,' came the reply.

Charlie, quite angry now, was determined to teach this upstart a lesson. 'Where is Noel Buntine?' he demanded in his best officer's voice.

'Under a truck the last time I saw him.'

Charlie marched over to a group of drivers standing beside the other road trains parked by the yards and demanded they point Noel Buntine out to him. They looked at him quizzically for a few seconds and one finally said, 'Jeez mate, that's him you was just talking to!'

Charlie walked sheepishly back across the yard to Noel who was still under the truck. 'Touché,' said Charlie.

'Whatever,' came the Aussie retort.

'I'm Charles Henderson, shall we start again?'

'I know who you bloody well are, Charlie!' Came the terse reply.

Charlie was at a loss for words for a few seconds. Noel, having finished the job, got out from under the truck, brushed the dust off his clothes and inadvertently all over Charlie's clean moleskins and highly polished riding boots, and said, 'I'm ready now to load those &&&¢%!* cattle of yours. Better get out of the way, Charlie, you might get dust on your boots.'

From that moment on Charlie thought Noel Buntine was the best. I won't print what Noel thought of Charlie. But each in their own inimitable way was a legend of the north. Noel because he was a doer, building a great

31

trucking company from scratch. Charlie because he created crazy dreams, most of which didn't work for him in his lifetime, but inspired other people to chase dreams.

The day Marlee and I drove into Katherine to attend Noel's funeral I received a fax from my publishers to tell me I was their best-selling author for 1993. I framed it! I was also second in *all* books sold in Australia for the year, with *Wild Swans* at number one. This was heady stuff!

We returned from Katherine, arriving home at around midnight. Another low settled in during the early hours of the morning and our road was finally closed for the rest of the wet season—about six weeks later than usual.

Danielle called the next night from New Zealand, 'Just called to tell you we are OK, and not to worry.'

'Why should I worry?' was my mystified reply.

'Mum, haven't you been watching TV?'

'Our receiver box is broken, what's happened!' I started to worry.

'There are terrible floods in the South Island, and we had to be airlifted out of Milford Sound by army helicopter last night.'

They certainly were having a honeymoon they wouldn't forget! I put the phone down, thankful they were safe and realising that not having TV had saved me days of endless worry.

As we are cut off by road at this time and our mail delivery is dependent on the weather, it can sometimes be up to a month before we see mail. So the phone, and more recently, the fax machine, are the only fast ways of contacting the station.

Around the middle of January I received a call asking me if I could be Australia Day Ambassador in one of the country towns in NSW as part of their celebrations. I was so disappointed I couldn't do this, but I had a conference already booked in Auckland, and there was no way I could get plane connections back to Australia in time.

After all the problems and delays I then experienced getting to this conference, I decided it was too risky to take bookings in the monsoon season, from mid December to March.

Two days before I was scheduled to leave for the conference not one, but three, low-pressure systems were either over, or approaching, Bullo, so I had to leave the station ahead of time. The young charter pilot who flew me to Kununurra had not been in the north long and this was his first wet season. He did a lot of map reading and looking out the window, trying to see landmarks in the breaks of heavy cloud cover. I did a lot of praying. I then had a three-hour wait for the jet to Darwin and another day in Darwin before my flight to New Zealand was due. All this because the lows approaching the station would make travelling in small planes impossible for several days. This meant it took the best part of a week of travelling for me to arrive in New Zealand and speak for one hour!

Weather again delayed my return flight into the station

and January was all but over when I unpacked my suitcase with two happy rottie puppies jumping all over me. Franz had given Marlee a delightful three-month-old, monster-size puppy called Bow, so we were now wall-to-wall with puppies, but they were lots of fun.

I suppose the major event of the month was the last payment of the miserable Trippe saga! This was the final payment of the legal fees for the Trippe court case. I had paid out the amount handed down in the judgment, my legal fees and now the last payment of his legal fees was due.

This was a very bitter–sweet moment in my life. Every month since August I had been making this monthly payment and I was sick to the stomach as this money went out of the bank account each time. But to have no reason for any further contact with this person was well worth the final payment.

I sent authority to my bank to transfer the funds, just transferring the round thousands figure and inadvertently leaving off two dollars.

Well, you should have seen the letter I received back from his lawyer, demanding that I pay the two dollars immediately, and what would happen to me if I didn't. Just the time taken to type the letter would have cost fifty times the amount! First I was amazed and then I got angry. To receive such a letter over two dollars after all the money I had paid over was too much!

In my anger I told my lawyer I wanted to reply in an even stronger tone. 'Up yours!', 'Get stuffed', 'Don't hold your breath waiting for it!', 'If you don't like it, sue me, you b......!' were some of my ideas. My lawyer told me to think it over and he would talk to me the next day. His advice was to just ignore it, no-one would be stupid enough to sue for $2!

I put all I wanted to say down on paper. I dearly wanted to send it but finally succumbed to sanity and filed it in the thick file marked 'Trippe'. I slammed the filing drawer shut and had the great satisfaction of being done with that unpleasant part of my life.

CHAPTER 3

February 1994 –
April 1994

*B*y the time I had unpacked, played with the
puppies, worked on only the very desperate office
work, caught up with station matters with Marlee, and
had a rare day to myself, it was time to leave again.

This was a short trip, only to Perth—just down the
road a bit, really. But unfortunately, it was home via
Melbourne, Sydney, and Darwin. I flew to Perth, arriving at 8 p.m. that night, spoke the next day and departed
for Melbourne, arriving at some unearthly hour of the
night. The following morning I was interviewed by a
board of directors to see if I was suitable to speak at their
company's conference the next year. We had a great
board meeting, and I must have passed the test—even
though I was dog tired—because the booking for the
conference was confirmed while I was flying to Darwin.

I was only home for nine days this time, then it was
off to Noumea. During the early years of learning to

control this 'fame' thing, I was never home for more than ten days at a time. So it was not unrealistic to predict that a conference engagement and a cyclone were bound to clash. They did!

The bad weather came in quickly. The front was approaching from the north-west tip of Western Australia from the Indian Ocean. Marlee, Franz and I had a weather conference and decided if I was to get out, Franz and I had better leave soon.

I hurriedly packed and we took off with the sky to the west getting blacker by the minute. As we flew up the coast, dark clouds rolled in at an alarming pace.

Halfway to Darwin, with still around forty minutes flying time, it didn't look good. We couldn't see the top of the clouds so we couldn't climb, or we would have ended up in the thick of it not being able to see, or running out of oxygen from being too high. The front was moving in so fast behind us that we couldn't go back, and it had moved so far inland we couldn't go south. Darwin weather, we were told, was still clear. We had nowhere to go but straight ahead and race the weather closing in all around us.

Thirty miles out, we were down to five hundred feet (when we usually fly at 2000 feet) and worried. We were flying through scattered cloud, with a solid ceiling of black above us. Identifying landmarks through the clouds was almost impossible, and we glimpsed the ground only now and then. Just around the area is a fairly wide hill which is a little higher than five hundred feet and we couldn't find it! Periodically we flew blind through flimsy clouds and really didn't want to come across the hill in those few seconds. Our eyes worked overtime, scanning the countryside and the ceiling seemed to get lower by the minute.

Franz checked regularly with Darwin where it was still fine with a cloud ceiling of one thousand feet. So we knew there was clear weather up ahead, if only we could just find that hill!

In the next ten minutes I experienced some record surges of adrenalin, right up there with the charging bull variety. I saw at least forty-five hills in that ten minutes, each sighting accompanied by an adrenalin surge and a few skipped heartbeats. Franz was working overtime following the direction of my frantically darting finger.

The cloud ceiling pushed us down to four-hundred feet—one hundred below the hilltop. We were running out of air space, fast. If we didn't break out of the bad weather soon, we would have to find a bush strip and land and there was still the dreaded hill to worry about.

'Look!' I pointed ahead, laughter bubbling over. The Daly River was just ahead of us which meant we had passed the hill somewhere back there in the murk. God knows how close we came to it, or if we came close at all.

As soon as we knew the hill was behind us, our problems vanished. Four hundred feet, with no five-hundred foot hill around, was suddenly a lot of air space. As we crossed the Daly River the bad weather parted like stage curtains to reveal Darwin further up ahead. As we circled the airport to land, the surrounding ocean sparkled in the sunlight—such a wonderful sight when you are up in a plane and want to land.

When I left for Sydney in a jet a few hours later, I

noticed the bad weather had arrived and Darwin was well and truly cloudbound. But the jet experienced just a few minutes of mild turbulence as it flew through the thick cloud layer, then broke out at around twenty thousand feet into bright sunshine. I didn't have to be a lookout or copilot on this flight so I relaxed.

When I accepted the conference in Noumea on the boat *Club Med II*, I did so because I thought it would mean only a short hop from Darwin over to New Caledonia. How wrong I was. Too late I found out that there are no flights out of Darwin to Noumea. To get there I had to fly Darwin–Sydney–Noumea. But it wasn't that bad as the conference was on board the *Club Med II* and involved cruising around the islands for four days. So I told my booking agent, 'Well, there are some things you just have to suffer ... I'll do it!'

It was a great conference with the whole boat taken over by the event. I spoke then had days of just enjoying the cruise. Rhonda Burchmore was on board and provided great entertainment just days before she flew to London for *Hot Shoe Shuffle*.

Whenever I set foot on board a boat the weather turns rough, and this time was no exception. The weather was pleasant during each day, but at night there was quite a swell. This was not enough to be bothersome to anyone except a dancer. But being the true professional she is, Rhonda put on a great show and we heard some great singing that night. With a London opening within the week, I know I would be worried about a lurching dance floor too!

Noumea airport didn't really have the facilities to

39

handle such a large group of tourists, and there were long lines and lots of waiting before our departure. In these situations I often tune in to the conversations around me. Two men in front of me were talking:

'Just look over there at our wives, they haven't drawn breath for half an hour!' said man number one.

'Gossiping,' was the reply of man number two.

'Yeh, I suppose you're right. They haven't seen each other since last night so I suppose they've got a lot to catch up on!'

They both laughed heartily. Then realising I was standing behind them turned and had the look of two little boys caught out. I smiled at them sweetly, but there was an awkward silence as they tried desperately to think of some way to explain their conversation.

I felt sorry for them so said, 'Your wives are not gossiping, they are networking.'

They smiled, relieved they had been let off the hook so lightly.

When they were joined by their wives, one wife said, 'I just mentioned to Betty you were looking for that travelling bag you saw advertised. You know that imported one you couldn't find anywhere? Well, Betty knows where we can get it! Isn't that great!'

Both women talked at once, bringing their husbands up to date on the information they had just exchanged.

The men listened dutifully, then as they were going through the door into customs they sheepishly turned around and looked at me, and I said, 'See, networking.'

They both smiled and disappeared through the door.

I arrived back at Bullo to days filled with office work, mounds of letters from readers and the operation of the station. I was also starting my next book *Some of My Friends Have Tails*. The manuscript wasn't due until March 1995 but the wet season is the only time I have free to write and I knew I wouldn't possible be able to get this book finished in the few months of the '95 wet season.

The problem with writing so far ahead of deadline is that there is no pressure to finish. I seem to work well under pressure and only write consistently when I am close to the handover date for a manuscript.

With twelve months up my sleeve, I was coasting along saying to myself, 'I'll start the book next week.'

Some days stories just start moving through my brain, and won't go away. I have learned in this short writing career of mine that is the time to stop whatever I am doing and write. If I ignore the story going through my brain, I regret it, because it is lost forever. So apart from some disconnected stories, I only had a sketchy outline of what form the next book would take. I knew I had to get into it soon, or I'd again be down to a few months with still half the book to go. Just looking at my diary told me the year was getting busier as it progressed.

The next conference was a very big, international one held at Darling Harbour in Sydney with over twenty speakers. On the first day all the speakers were asked to go to the green room and arrange the electronic side of their presentation with the technicians. Mine was simple. I was just going to show slides as I talked about Bullo. But some speakers were combining slides, videos, and other machines for graphs. As we sat waiting for a technician to become available, I busied myself jotting down questions I wanted to ask about the company and watching people—my favourite pastime. A man walked over to me—the only female speaker—and in a very thick American accent said, 'Ah have mah coffee strong, Ah don't like instant, and Ah have one sugar and a little skim milk, thanks. When Ah'm here waiting each day, Ah like a coffee about every three hours, but don't bother keeping track, Ah'll just tell you when Ah need it.

'Could Ah have a cup now, please.' And he walked off to direct a technician, but not before glancing back at me, with the expression of, 'Why are you still sitting there, get mah coffee.'

I couldn't help thinking, I pity your poor wife. I found the refreshments in the next room and noticed the other men taking care of their own coffee. I returned to the room and put the perculated coffee next to our American who hardly noticed the delivery, as all his attention was focused on the technician. I received an officious 'Thank you' as I went back to my chair.

After lunch I looked up and my American was descending upon me again. 'Oh dear,' I thought, 'not again.' But this time he looked upset and extremely flustered. I was sure this order would be for a double Scotch.

I have to pause here to set the scene. I consider speaking on the circuit as an off the farm job, not my complete career. I enjoy meeting people immensely, I would never tire of that part, I just hate standing up in front of an audience and speaking. Even after all these years, and I don't know how many speeches, I still get nervous and am only happy when it is over. But full-time professional speakers are very dedicated and keen to be the best. This American guy put a questionnaire on every seat in the convention centre—about twelve hundred people attended—asking the delegates where they would rank his speech out of the twenty-five speakers. This was followed by a whole page of questions.

So having given you this inside information, you might find the following exchange as amusing as I did. He continued his flustered approach. Gone was Mr Efficiency: he stammered, he stumbled, he bumbled. The cause of all this? He had just found out he had instructed the keynote speaker to get his coffee.

He blustered on and finally managed to blurt out, 'Ah thought you were the tea lady!' in a truly agonising moan.

I tried to put him out of his misery by saying, 'Please, stop worrying, this is such a minor thing, you didn't upset me in the least.'

But he didn't seem to hear and continued his tirade. I then mustered together my most official tone, looked seriously into his eyes, and said, 'I can assure you ...' a long pause followed to get his attention, 'if I didn't want to get you coffee, I wouldn't have been the least bit embarrassed to tell you.'

I continued staring intently and he backed away, thanking me and bobbing repeatedly as he retreated. In the professional world of speaking, he had apparently just committed a cardinal sin!

It must be something with Americans and me. The next one I met was also a speaker at the conference. As I waited to hand my slides over to the technician for my presentation, I watched as this guy ran up and down the rows placing the questionnaires on each seat. I was immediately reminded of Mr Efficiency. Once he'd finished, he walked over to me, put out his hand and welcomed me to the conference and handed me a questionnaire. He told me he was speaking midweek, would *love* me to attend his session and would be *mighty* pleased if I would fill in the questionnaire afterwards. Then with the widest smile to come out of the Americas, he said, 'Do you think you could do that for little ol' me?'

In my sweetest American accent I told him I couldn't because I was also a speaker and I was opening the conference and would unfortunately be gone before he spoke.

The shock registered, he didn't say it, but I could read his mind clearly, and it was saying, 'But you're a woman ... Opening speaker and you're a woman!'

He could see I knew what he was thinking by my smile, so he hurriedly departed.

The next morning I was sitting in the green room having coffee when in he came.

'I've been doing some research on you.' He went on to give me a rundown on the business side of my life. I think he had to do this to justify in his mind why I was guest speaker. Then he said he'd spoken to his wife on the phone, and said, 'Guess what, the opening speaker is this woman who lives on a cattle station in the Outback.'

His wife's reply was, 'Oh I've read her book and if she speaks as well as she writes, you're dead.'

This remark stemmed back to the questionnaires and how the audience rates the speakers. This seems to be the important factor most times Americans speak.

So, as you can imagine, his wife's remark had him worried. 'Have you written a book called *From Strength to Strength*?' he asked hesitantly.

When I replied, 'Yes, I have,' he walked away quite crestfallen.

When I walked offstage after my speech and a lengthy question time, he walked over to me and shook hands and told me it was a great story to listen to. He said he was going out to buy all my books, and that his wife was right, he was dead!

Marlee's shoulder was still really causing her trouble and her doctor said she needed at least a week of regular, daily work by a physio to get the shoulder on a recovery path. So the first week of April found Marlee in Darwin and Franz venturing out on the road for the first time since December, leaving Jacqui and me to hold the fort.

The wet season was officially over on Bullo with the last light storm around the beginning of March. During the season we had lots of bad weather and low clouds but no heavy falls of rain. Franz had decided to try to drive out our road, not just for a joy-ride—mind you he was very excited—he was off to pick up a brand new hay baler.

If you saw the baler we had been working with, you would understand his excitement. When Dick Wicks, alias 'Uncle Dick'—our mechanic in the seventies and eighties—saw this baler heading towards the workshop, he went crosseyed. At just the mention of it he would disappear on a bender, sometimes for months, hoping that when he returned the hay baling would be over and the dreaded machine would be sitting in the shed. This dread passed onto Franz and any other mechanic we had here during its time. The previous year Franz and a fairly cluey mechanic did some extensive work on the terrible baler. The verdict was it would do the job that season, but would need to be replaced soon or thrown on the junk heap. This was something Uncle Dick, then Franz, had dearly wanted to do many times. Franz had spent more time inside it clearing blockages of hay and in the workshop fixing it than he had out in the field using it. So in March when the rains stopped, the skies cleared and the hay crop swayed in the gentle breeze and was ready to harvest, thoughts had turned once more to the dreaded baler!

We had planted double the acreage this year so there was a lot of hay to harvest. Calculating the time for our very slow machine to bale all the hay, plus time for breakdowns, it was obvious we couldn't get it done.

Franz called from Timber Creek after he had made it out on our road and said the road was in fairly good condition. There were quite a few wash aways, he got bogged a few times but he thought those areas would dry out by the time he returned. It would be a slow trip back towing the baler from Katherine and he was also driving up to Darwin to pick up Marlee.

For the week after their return we saw nothing on TV except the video on the baling machine. When Franz learns about something new, he really covers the subject. And during hay-baling season we had a very happy Franz—he returned to the house each day with a broad grin on his face due to no breakdowns and hay bale numbers ticking up at an amazing rate.

With the month ticking by it was time to start the mustering season. Marlee was onto the grader and out fixing up the road the morning after they arrived home, and when she wasn't grading was on the phone interviewing the new team for the season. We had fencing to be done, the hay to cart and stockpile, lots of machines to service before the season and cattle to muster.

The phone was running hot because I was off on two book tours in May so there were endless phone calls from radio stations and newspapers all around Australia and New Zealand. These were interviews arranged by my publishers to give advance notice that I would be in a particular town the next month. Even with all this publicity I still get letters after I return from these exhausting coast-to-coast tours, saying, 'I missed you when you came to our town. I didn't know you were here. I'm so disappointed I missed you!' This amazes me when you look at the pages of publicity appointments I do in the months leading up to the launch of one of my books.

Marlee's birthday found her grading the road, but that Sunday she had breakfast in bed and I cooked a birthday lunch and dinner for her for a change.

I was leaving for Sydney at the end of April for a round of conferences, a few days with my sister Sue in Caloundra then book tours around Australia and New Zealand and would not be home until the end of May. But in the three weeks before I left what I had to achieve in the form of work was near impossible. But I started anyhow. In the middle of this intensive program of interviews and office work I had a quick trip to Perth for a conference, then it was back home to more interviews, work and packing for a month on the road, or in the air, I should say.

Having travelled extensively for three years I was now sick of the sight of suitcases, and had vowed to myself I would take only one suitcase on this trip, no matter what! But the big problem with going around Australia in May is that you need clothes for three seasons. Then I had to consider the South Island of New Zealand which meant packing some woollens. Out the door went my one suitcase vow!

This tour was for the sequel, the dreaded sequel. I had no idea if this book, *The Strength in Us All*, was any good; I never do. I always wait and first watch my publishers' reaction, then the readers'. It's a painful process for me—much like having a baby. There are the months of long hours of work to produce the manuscript, then more months of work with the editor. This is followed by months of worry about what I haven't put in and what I should have changed. Then there's the long wait for printing and finally you have the finished book in your hands.

Then the worry starts all over again. What will the reviews say? But most importantly, will people like it? Will it sell?

So it ends up being more like the pregnancy of an elephant!

The curse of the sequel had me really worried and the record was not good as far as I could see. The words, 'Oh there's a second book out, but it's nowhere as good as the first!' gave me nightmares. So the sooner I started this tour the better. I would soon know if I was about to join the ranks of writers of dud sequels or if the second book would be as popular as *From Strength to Strength*.

April was also time for Marlee's six-monthly check-up after her cancer operation. Marlee had been diagnosed with cancer of the cervix in 1992. The cancer was discovered at a very early stage and the doctors were convinced that her operation had removed every trace, but a check-up every six months for the first three years was necessary, after which it could be yearly. Six months comes around very quickly and we'd no sooner get over the relief of an 'all clear' in one check-up than start worrying about the next appointment.

So Marlee flew me to Darwin. I had the nervewracking wait for her check-up to deal with along with sequel jitters. Not to mention the thought of tours in two countries. I kissed her goodbye, told her to call me the moment she had the results, then gave her an extra hug—any excuse to delay my leaving. I brushed tears away as I assured her I was fighting fit and raring to go, when in truth I just wanted to go home with her, so daunting seemed the month's challenges ahead of me.

When I arrived in Sydney I was whisked off to the ABC to meet all the finalists of the ABC Rural Woman of the Year as I was speaking at the awards presentation that night. I then rushed across town to a recording studio to record a radio fund appeal for the MS Society.

After a forty-five-minute turnaround at my hotel I arrived at the Rural Woman of the Year awards presentation. We had a great night and it was very satisfying to see those capable women who have contributed so much to the land and this country being acclaimed at long last.

I finally laid my weary head on the pillow at 1.30 a.m., having just completed a twenty-one-and-a-half-hour day. I drifted off to sleep hoping there wouldn't be too many more days like it, but knowing in the back of my mind I was wrong—I had seen my book-tour itinerary.

The following morning I boarded a flight for Brisbane. By lunchtime I was sitting on the verandah at Susan's house, looking at one of my favourite views, down that peaceful creek and out to sea. I rested and slept for two days, reorganised my suitcase, and was ready for the starter's gun when I hugged Sue and Ralph goodbye on the 30th.

CHAPTER 4

May
1994

*E*ach time I venture on a book tour I think this time
will be easier. But this was my third tour and it
wasn't getting any easier. The tours were getting longer!
This tour of New Zealand and Australia was twenty-five
days.

People often ask me if I find the tours exhausting, and
if so why do I do them. I look on the tours as a guide
to how people feel about my books, and, I suppose, me.
So the longer the tour the better, in my eyes, as I get
to meet the people who read my books. It would be
awful to go on tour and no-one wanted to meet you!
So I never complain about the volume of work entailed,
I just keep very fit, going into training a few months
before. So far this has worked and I have lasted the
distance!

The tour around New Zealand was no exception. In
six days I travelled almost the full length of the North

and South Islands, from Auckland to Dunedin and back, zigzagging in planes and cars, not to mention attending twenty-six public appearances. But this was just the baby tour compared to what was coming up! When I'm on tour I speak to Marlee daily—usually late at night or first thing in the morning. We mostly talk about the station operation and how my tour is progressing. During one of these conversations, towards the end of my New Zealand tour, Marlee gave me the good news that her check-up was clear and she now only needed yearly tests. I know how that news made me feel, so I can only just begin to imagine what it meant to Marlee. I flew out of Auckland, headed for Sydney, with a happy heart.

The Australian tour was the King Kong of book tours—nineteen days with a twenty-nine-page itinerary. There were twenty-seven phone interviews before I left Bullo and another fifteen on tour. Along with twenty literary lunches and dinners, twenty-six studio radio interviews, fifteen newspaper articles, seven bookshop signings and eight TV appearances, we had Mike Munro and a TV crew following us for a few days in Queensland.

I have all my itineraries filed away. I'm not sure why, perhaps as memories to treasure in my older years. I'll probably look at them when I'm eighty and shake my head and say, 'How did I do that?' Although I won't have to wait till I'm eighty: I ask that now!

Even though each tour is basically the same, each has its own special events. The first day in Queensland was full of appointments and finished with a small literary dinner for 150 guests. The itinerary listed a 7 p.m. start and a 9.30 finish. I thought this was a bit ambitious, but we were in the country, so I guessed early start, early finish.

One of my guardian angels, Jane—otherwise known as my publicist—was not arriving until the following day, so the local Pan Macmillan sales rep was my guide. Not that she could have changed events, they were very much out of our hands.

One small thing turned the entire evening upside down. The gas stove, on which the dinner was to be cooked, stopped working. So the 9.30 departure time found me just sitting down to dinner. My eight o'clock speech was struggling for a ten thirty slot by which time most of the men had moved into the bar and were very rowdy.

When I finally got up to speak the noise was rolling out from the bar. One of the few remaining men in the room disappeared into the bar, and in a few seconds the rest of the men quietly returned to their seats and we got on with the night's proceedings. I arrived back at the hotel at 12.30 and drifted off to sleep thinking, 'Thank heavens Jane will arrive tomorrow,' while drowsily assuring myself, 'Bad start, good finish!'

The next day it was on to the Gold Coast and the Sheraton Mirage where we were met by Mike Munro and a crew from *A Current Affair*. They were going to follow me around for a few days to film a segment on life on the road with an author. As nervous as I was to have a

TV camera trained on me most of my waking moments, I was grateful for such fantastic coverage.

The crew were a great group of guys, helpful and considerate. When four hundred women descended upon me at the Gold Coast literary luncheon, they were amazed at first, then once over the shock, pitched in and did anything they could to help. And Mike Munro was, well, what can I say? There are not many times in my life I have wished to be younger, but after a few days on the road with Mike, I wished I was thirty years younger, a lot slimmer, a lot prettier, a lot . . . Well, you get the picture, I don't have to spell it out. What a charmer!

Mike did throw me one curved ball at the luncheon, however, not that he would know this, as his request seemed quite reasonable. Luckily, because of an embarrassing situation on my first tour, I was partly prepared. During question time at the first dinner of the first book tour, I was asked if I would recite the verse in the front of *From Strength to Strength*.

I suppose most people think that every word of a book is engraved in an author's brain forever. Maybe this is the case with some authors, but with me, the moment I write something down it goes out of my mind, like a train dropping off passengers at a station.

When I wrote the verse at the beginning of *From Strength to Strength*, it was at the request of my editor. She wanted a verse of five or six lines that related to the story and could I fax it through in the hour, was the next request. The manuscript was ready to go to the printers, it was just waiting on the verse.

So I scribbled, crossed out and scribbled for an hour, came up with a verse I was satisfied with, then faxed it. I filed my copy with the rest of the manuscript and promptly forgot about it ... until that moment! I stared out at the audience in horror nine months after I had hastily written, faxed, filed and forgotten it!

So I just said, 'I can't remember how it starts, give me the first few words.'

I had no idea what I was going to do if that didn't prompt my memory. There was a rustle through the audience as books were produced from bags around the room, and a chorus came to me. 'Create a dream ...' Then silence, as they waited.

Luckily it all came back to me and I finished the verse convincing everyone I *had* written it. I learned my lesson, though, and so the verse beginning the second book was engraved on my brain as I started out on the tour.

Never did I dream Mike Munro would ask me to recite it on national television, but that's the way it happened. We were sitting eating lunch when all the cameras zoomed in on me, making me more nervous than usual, and so the recital wasn't word perfect. I rearranged a few words, but on the whole it wasn't too bad.

An extremely good interview with Mike, a great sequence on the beach at sunrise and the literary lunch-eon all made for a very watchable *A Current Affair* program.

Staying at the Sheraton Mirage had me remembering a fortunate escape I had had from a disastrous resort business venture a few years earlier. I had received a phone call from a man representing a large company interested in building luxury resorts in the Kimberley area. They were looking with some interest at Bullo and wondered if the company's director could come to the station and discuss some ideas with me. Always looking out for an opportunity to pay off Charlie's debts, I said yes. The appointment was made for the middle of the following month and we got on with our busy life. A week before the appointment I had a note in my diary to call and see if everything was still as arranged. It was.

The day of the meeting arrived and Marlee and I spent the morning in the kitchen cooking a special meal. The arrangement was that the company director would arrive by private jet at 11.30. When no-one had arrived by 1.30 the stockmen pounced on the lunch with delight.

The next morning I was still fuming and decided I would definitely not do business with such people and would call and tell them why. The phone was answered with a very rude, 'What!'

I was taken aback by the tone—this was one angry man—but perservered, reminding him of the failure to keep the appointment. I asked if there was a reason and took a deep breath and waited.

Well, I heard more four-letter words in the next minute than I knew existed then had the phone slammed down in my ear.

In amongst all the swearing, a sketchy story emerged. The company had gone to the wall and our VIP visitor had vanished. The man I spoke to had lost all the money

56

he had invested and was worried he might lose even more.

That evening Marlee and I sat down to the evening news and the name of our mystery guest was soon revealed. We suddenly understood why his man in the Kimberley was so rude and how very lucky we were to have escaped the whole sordid mess.

Sitting under a large company sign was a receptionist telling the reporter she didn't know how Mr Skase could be contacted or when he would be in the office. Yes, the company coming to lunch was Qintex and the VIP who didn't turn up in the private jet, who knows!

Marlee and I just looked at each other for a while in silence and thanked our lucky stars we didn't get mixed up in that mess.

Over the years I have had many occasions to silently repeat the thanks and it taught me a lesson: whenever a company calls to present a business idea, the first thing I do is check up on them. Charlie taught me this a long time ago and I had just forgotten.

I left the memories and the Mirage behind and headed for Brisbane and dinner with 550 people at the Sheraton, had breakfast with another three hundred Brisbanites and several radio, newspaper and TV appointments before departing to Armidale.

Country towns are always go, go, go on a book tour and this one was no exception. By the time I kicked off my shoes in the hotel room I'd survived a seventeen-hour day. At least my doubts about this book not being as well received as the first book were beginning to fade.

The following day we flew to Sydney for a literary luncheon for 710 people. The demand was such my publishers had been asked if I could squeeze in an extra dinner to accommodate all the people turned away from the lunch. So a dinner was arranged for two nights later.

But first there was Friday the 13th to get through! It was Charlie's lucky day, he always told me, never giving a reason why. At the beginning of each year, he always put a special mark on any Friday the 13th on the calendar, then tried his hardest to arrange big deals on any of those dates. Not that it helped any of the deals he managed to schedule!

This Friday the 13th was very special because I was flying to Palm Beach for a literary lunch in a De Havilland Beaver, the same as our dear old Bertha. The fifteen-minute flight was crowded with memories, with the added thrill of taking off from Rose Bay and landing in Pittwater.

Flying in a dear old Beaver after seventeen years was such a thrill. They have such a distinctive sound and I can recognise the sound of the radial engine anywhere. I heard it so often in the pre-dawn between 1974 and 1980. Particularly in the winter months, Charlie would take off in the dark, when the air was extremely cold so he could lift the maximum payload. Of course Charlie's idea of the maximum payload was twice the legal load allowed for the plane! Cold air enables an engine to lift more load because the air has more density. An engine develops less power in hot air and at high altitudes where there is less oxygen.

The sound of Bertha labouring to get Charlie and his

load airborne is forever etched in my mind. I would stand in the kitchen listening, and repeat over and over in my mind, 'Come on, girl, you can do it!'

By the time she passed the homestead, still on the ground after three quarters of a mile, the chant would be an urgent, 'Come on, girl! Come on!' The sound of the big engine would blast into the homestead with a furious, 'Whaaaaa' as she tried so hard to do the job.

With a normal load, Bertha would lift off level with the homestead, but it was very rare she lifted off with such a load! Instead, she would roar to the end of the airstrip and struggle into the air when she ran out of runway. Barely fifty feet above the ground, she would just maintain air speed and flying low over the salt flats until disappearing from sight, still trying to obtain some height.

One time Charlie loaded her with so much meat he had to fly all the way to Port Keats—up the Victoria River, then along the coastline—over water because Bertha had no power left to climb and could only go straight ahead. Charlie's only comments were that he had a bit of trouble with a few small hills and tall trees on the approach to the Port Keats airstrip, and that the stall button wouldn't stop beeping and annoyed him.

It seemed fitting to be flying in such a plane on Friday the 13th, circling over the house where Charlie died, then landing in Pittwater where he lived onboard his boat, moored right near where the plane lands. If Charlie wasn't pulling the strings to control the events of that day, I just don't know. It felt like he'd written the itinerary!

It was back to Sydney and more work and by the

time I ticked off my last appointment it was another seventeen-hour day, but a truly memorable one.

After travelling through as many country towns as possible in three days it was on to Melbourne and multiple radio, television and newspaper interviews.

I am forever surprised at the wide scope of questions I am asked. There is one question, however, I get regularly: 'And where do you live now?'

I don't know why it is assumed that now I am a so-called celebrity I would naturally have moved to the city. After being asked this question for the fourth or fifth time, I was a bit tired of replying, 'On the station,' and varied the answer to 'In a 747 jet'.

Seeing I had just told the young reporter I had been travelling for much of the last ten months and had spent little time at home, I assumed he would get the joke. But like a lot of new reporters he just concentrated on headlines.

His eyebrows shot up in amazement. 'You have your own 747? You live in a plane?'

I quickly explained it was a joke, as I could already see the next day's headlines!

I think the main reason I am able to get through these gruelling tours is because of my ability to sleep anywhere. I can board a plane and be asleep before it leaves the ground. On one flight from Melbourne to Hobart I fell asleep while the plane was delayed on the tarmac before take-off. I opened my eyes as we were taxiing and turned to Jane and said, 'That was a quick flight.'

She shook her head in amazement and said, 'We haven't left Melbourne yet.'

I considered this a bonus and went back to sleep.

Cars are no different. When we drove to Frankston— a lengthy drive out of Melbourne—I fell asleep almost immediately, sleeping until the car went over a speed hump as we approached our destination at the Country Club. I turned to Jane and said, 'Gee, that was a rough landing!'

She looked at me with concern until I got my bearings and realised we were in a car, not a plane.

Victoria and Tasmania went along nicely with enjoyable dinners, luncheons, store signings and meeting people in the thousands. As I was travelling from east to west around the country, Bryce Courtenay was going from west to east with his latest book. We crossed paths on a television show on which they advertised every household item you could think of.

The woman hosting the show was amazing. She displayed and disposed of the products so quickly, anything unbreakable was thrown over her shoulders as the camera zoomed in on the next item held in her other hand. People were crawling around on the floor behind the chairs removing packets so they didn't pile up above chair level.

The show was like an assembly line with the guests lined up offstage and pushed, one at a time, into the spotlight, being wired for sound as they were bustled into the interviewing chair. The host would flash them a beautiful smile, fire a few questions in their direction, wave some products around, then thank them for coming. As the cameras moved off the stunned guest, the sound man would rush them offstage, grab the microphone and wire the next guest.

When we'd just arrived I was standing at the end of the line and saw Bryce Courtenay leaving the set. I'm sorry I missed that interview, as the last thing Bryce would have been was dazed. He probably started selling the products for the host! As he was passing he let out a loud welcoming, 'Sara!', gave me a bear hug and said it was great to see me again, and was gone!

Jane looked fairly surprised and said, 'I didn't know you knew Bryce Courtenay!'

'Neither did I,' I replied. 'We were introduced at a conference recently, but I didn't think he would remember me.'

Recovering from my bear hug I watched as the guest before me was being interviewed. He was a magician performing at a local club and he had with him a lovely white rabbit, which sat on his lap during his brief interview.

The magician was whisked away and I was wired and rushed to the chair. I sat down and immediately jumped up, as the rabbit was still on the chair. The magician was rushed offstage so fast he'd left his rabbit. The cameras were panning in on the scene and I was being hissed at to sit! It was evident they were running behind schedule. Behind the lights was someone intimating the same and a third person was dramatically holding up a hand with fingers disappearing at an alarming rate.

No-one was heading onstage to take the rabbit and

I had to sit down, so I picked it up and put it on my lap and waited for the cameras, smiling and stroking the rabbit. While the cameras were on the host doing a speedy introduction, the rabbit was whisked away by its owner. After a few rushed questions I was also whisked away and in record time found myself outside the building. All I can say about that interview is, 'Whew!'

Another amusing experience occurred at a book-signing session at David Jones in Melbourne. The store had put up a very big display just inside the main entrance with huge posters of the book's cover. I was surrounded by these at a large desk with a sign over my head which read, 'Come and meet Sara Henderson'.

After a busy few hours of signing books I was sitting back massaging my signing hand when an elderly, well dressed gentleman approached. He leaned over the desk and in a quiet, confidential tone asked, 'What floor underpants?'

I looked at him with a dazed expression. 'What?'

With an annoyed expression he glanced both ways to check no-one was listening, and hissed a little louder, 'Men's underwear! What floor?'

I had recovered sufficiently by this time to say I had no idea.

Upon which he stepped back and in a loud sergeant-major voice demanded to know why.

I told him, while pointing to the posters surrounding me, that I was there to sign books.

Very angry by now, he told me I should sit some-where else—not at the information desk—and marched away.

Even with all these funny situations the same pressures are always present on tour. I don't think I will ever eliminate the stress, but in some situations it does have a bizarre effect on me. On one occasion after speaking to a crowd of six hundred and signing what felt like several books for every person present, Jane handed me a book belonging to the woman who had organised the function and asked me to sign it. I wrote her name, signed my signature and was about to hand back the book, when Jane said, 'Say, "thank you".'

So I did.

Jane looked at me with a concerned expression and said patiently, 'Write, "thank you"!'

The rest of the twenty-six days were pretty much the same as the other tours—lots of travelling, meeting loads of lovely people, sleeping in a lot of strange beds, and not having a clue where I was most of the time. No, it would probably be fair to say, all the time!

Midway through the tour Franz flew to America with Jim Hazelton to purchase a Cessna 185 tail-dragger for the station. For non-flying buffs, that's a small six-seater aircraft. Jim Hazelton came into our lives in 1993 when he arrived on Bullo with Dick Smith and Dick's wife, Pip. We had been in contact with him ever since, talking mostly about airplanes and fishing.

We had been hiring an aircraft for months and the convenience of having a plane full time on the station was spoiling us. So we started looking for a smaller version of the old Beaver. We needed a plane that was rugged, had high-lift wing, could lift a good payload (although not in the Charlie category) and could be reliable on bush landing strips. Marlee and Franz told me such a plane was a Cessna 185 tail-dragger, but they were as scarce as hen's teeth in Australia, particularly in good condition. There were a lot of 'ifs' involved: If we did find one, it would be very expensive. The next 'if' was if the owner was willing to part with it, so cherished are these planes.

Jim Hazelton said we would be able to get a very good one in America: all we had to do was fly it back to Australia. Jim was starting to sound surprisingly like Charlie! Although it might have something to do with being a pilot as Franz and Marlee didn't think there was anything particularly amazing in this idea.

So Franz and Jim wandered around the mid-western states of America, looking at tail-draggers as I wandered around Australia signing books and Marlee was mustering at Bullo.

Many faxes were sent in a circle between Franz in America, Marlee on the station, and me at a different hotel every night. If the bank manager wanted to ask a question or get my authority, he could only go through Marlee as I left the hotels at 5 a.m. each morning and Marlee had my dreaded itinerary.

Marlee called one night to say Franz and Jim had found our plane. It had a gold-medal seal and only fifteen hours on the engine. The plane was in immaculate condition and belonged to a plane-crazy guy, so had every accessory you could imagine. I was about to forward the funds when Franz in his usual exacting manner went over the plane from tail to propeller with a fine-tooth comb.

The owner assured Franz he was wasting his time as the engine was in top-class condition and the plane had gold-medal seal approval. Franz is not one easily swayed from his track so he continued his inspection and took out the oil filters. When he removed the second filter he found shavings. Fine metal shavings signify normal engine wear, but if larger shavings are found it indicates something is amiss. What Franz found in the second filter was larger than 'fine'. After a thorough inspection, a fracture was found in the crankshaft! The owner couldn't apologise enough and offered to replace the crankshaft. But the thought of how close they had come to engine failure over the Pacific wouldn't leave Franz and Jim's minds.

The second plane of their choice didn't have as many accessories, wasn't finished in leather, didn't belong to a plane-crazy buff, but its second oil filter came up clear! That was the all-important test when you had fifty hours of flying over the Pacific Ocean in front of you. For a second time the bank was geared up to transfer funds but this time they went through and we were now the proud owners of a 185 tail-dragger.

Our little plane came from Eveleth, Minnesota. In his journey to find and finally purchase this plane, Franz and Jim had flown to Sydney, Los Angeles, San Francisco,

Seattle, Idaho, Minnesota, Denver and to Torrance, Palo Alto (where they got an export permit) and Oakland in California. From San Francisco Franz travelled to Hawaii by commercial jet as there was so much fuel to carry to get the little plane over this longest stretch— just over thirteen hours—there was only room for one person in the cockpit. So Jim flew this leg alone with the copilot's seat occupied by a fuel tank.

Franz joined him in Hilo, Hawaii and flew the little plane to Christmas Island, Pago Pago, Norfolk Island, Lord Howe Island and Kempsey where he dropped Jim home. Finally he flew to Sydney's Bankstown Airport where the plane had to stay for a few weeks to go through inspection so it could be listed on the Australian register and receive its new Australian call sign (or its registration number, similar to a car's number plate). Franz left the plane there and flew to Darwin where he was met by Marlee and they drove back to the station in the truck. And I thought I had done a lot of travelling in nineteen days!

I had arrived home on the morning of the 25th May, the same day the little plane was leaving Oakland, California on its long journey to its new home in the outback of Australia. Marlee and I followed the entire flight, living it by the hour. In the atlas we marked the route across the ocean and expected times of arrival for each touchdown. It seemed such a long way for such a tiny plane! We watched the clock and stood over the phone when an e.t.a. had passed and the phone hadn't rung.

When they arrived on Christmas Island after a smooth

flight, the biggest problem was finding a phone to call us. We had some of the most worrying hours of our life just staring at the minute speck in the middle of the Pacific Ocean in the atlas, hoping with all our hearts Franz and Jim were on it! Christmas Island is not much more than a fuel stop in the middle of the Pacific Ocean. There are not many other facilities there apart from the fuel.

Everything that needed to be done to get ready for a very early start the next morning took an extraordinary length of time. It was midnight before they could find a phone and a tired Franz opened with the words we were longing to hear, 'Hello, Franz here.'

The next leg to Pago Pago in American Samoa was nearly ten hours. When Franz and Jim were a few hours out of Christmas Island they picked up a 747 cargo plane on their radio, it was flying from Florida to Pago Pago. Franz told them he couldn't pick up Pago Pago on the radio and asked them to relay his e.t.a. in Pago Pago and his current position.

The pilot passed on the information. Not long after he came back to double-check Franz's e.t.a. He wanted to know what Franz was flying as his e.t.a. was in another seven hours. He just wanted to make sure Franz was in an aircraft! The speed of a 747 would be around 360 knots, while Franz and Jim were floating along at around 130 knots, depending on which way the wind was blowing! When Franz told him they were flying a Cessna 185 from Minnesota to Australia, the pilot said they were crazy and gave Franz his contact number in Pago Pago. He wanted to take them out to dinner as he just had to meet people crazy enough to do what they were doing. He couldn't believe they were flying across the ocean in a small single-engine plane!

Seven hours later he picked them up at the airport and took them to dinner. It was a long night as he listened to Franz talk about the destination of the little plane from Minnesota—a half a million acre cattle station in the outback of Australia. They parted friends and he promised to come and visit Bullo if his cargo plane ever ended up in Darwin.

When you register a plane you can choose your own call sign. Franz gave them SBH—my initials—so our new little plane was registered VH-SBH. But maybe we should have christened her VH-CEH—Charlie's initials—because sitting here now, looking at the transfer papers, I see the date of purchase was Friday the 13th May! So while I was flying to Palm Beach in a Beaver, on the other side of the world Franz was taking delivery of our plane.

Information about the sales of *The Strength in Us All* was coming in by the end of May. The book hit the bestseller list the first week of its release and on the 18th May in the *Bulletin*'s top ten bestsellers, *The Strength in Us All* was listed number one, with *From Strength to Strength* at number two. I definitely put that magazine away in my treasure box!

Both books stayed on the bestseller lists for a few

months, which dispelled my fears about the sequel. In fact *The Strength in Us All* sold around 89,000 copies in ten days, which was a record at the time.

May from start to finish was full of challenge, excitement and triumph. What a month it was!

CHAPTER 5

June 1994–
August 1994

June found us back together at Bullo for nine days. The mustering was in full swing and after a few days of relaxing I tackled the work piling up in the office. It was then off to Sydney again.

This year I had again missed a holiday during the wet season and had no breaks ahead of me until December. I was certainly doing very poorly with this management of my life idea! June had the potential to develop the same breathtaking pace as May and I couldn't do a thing about it—it was already down in the diary!

I was in Sydney this time for the Australian Book Fair. James wanted me to sign books at the Pan Macmillan stand. I had never been to a book fair and thought it would be an interesting part of the publishing business to observe. A big attraction for me was that there were American publishers there. My big dream has always been to get my first book into the American market! If this happened, I could surely retire!

Midmorning the first day James had some bad news. 'Now don't worry,' were his first words, so of course I immediately started worrying. He told me there was a rumour going around the fair a book was being offered to publishers giving Charlie's side of the story in response to my first book. This, I thought, was quite bizarre considering he had been dead for eight years. Who could give Charlie's side of the story, except Charlie? There was no book written yet, just feelers out for money in advance to write a book. Now why didn't that surprise me?

There is easy money involved in riding on the coat-tails of a bestseller. Apparently publishers sometimes buy a negative manuscript about one of their bestselling authors just to keep it off the market. I asked James not to offer a penny. We would wait.

The rest of the day passed gloomily as I fought the emotions that surged through my body. James said to forget about it, which was easier said than done! He said he would keep a finger on the pulse and come back to me as soon as he heard anything. He was right, of course, but there was a constant rumbling in the back of my head I was having trouble dismissing.

The main reason I was in Sydney was that *From Strength to Strength* was on the shortlist for the Australian Booksellers' Book of the Year Award. The awards dinner was that night so I decided not to let the nasty incident spoil this exciting night for me.

Of course when I had first seen the list of books a few months before much of the excitement had faded. The other nine books were quite outstanding and I was honoured just to be listed.

The Australian Book Awards include awards for non-fiction, fiction, poetry, publisher of the year, bookseller of the year, and so on. This was the first year of the Australian Book of the Year award.

The time for the awards finally arrived during the dinner. The list was up on the screen and it looked pretty daunting. There I was, right down the bottom at number ten! About the right position against all those titles was my first thought. Some of the books had been around for a long time, others had won top awards. My book was up against the likes of *Cloudstreet* by Tim Winton, *Remembering Babylon* by David Malouf, *Patrick White—A Life* by David Marr and *My Place* by Sally Morgan. I was laughing to myself by the time I reached this far down the list, but it continued with *A Fence Around the Cuckoo* by Ruth Park and *The Road from Coorain* by Jill Ker Conway! Yes, I said to myself, you're in the right place there, my girl, tenth! Still, I reasoned with myself, being in the top ten was not bad, considering I was in the company of some of the great Australian books.

'Sara!' Jeannine, Pan Macmillan's publicity director, was shaking my shoulder.

'What?' I answered, lost in deep thought.

'It's your book, you've won!'

A spotlight zoomed in on me sitting at the table lost in my reverie, with Jeannine repeating, 'Your book has won!'

I couldn't move or think. Now I truly know what the expression 'like a stunned mullet' means!

All the recipients of the other awards had gone on stage with a speech clutched in their hand. When I had first seen the other books listed, I'd decided not to worry about writing a speech, so as I walked towards the stage, I screamed at my brain to start thinking. But my brain was blown away by the events of the previous few minutes and all it could do was repeat, 'What an honour! What an honour!' I kept pleading with it to give me more. I needed a speech! But when I reached the microphone my brain was still on its chant, so my first words were, 'What an honour!' Then the very original, 'This is something I certainly didn't expect,' I stared into the audience, close to tears.

The clapping stopped and the audience sat waiting. I pleaded with my brain to produce something and the audience kept waiting. On the speaking circuit, like all speakers, I had always dreaded experiencing a mental block. A few times when speaking I had forgotten the question I was answering, but this had presented no problem, as I just asked the audience to repeat the question and I was back on track. This was different. My brain was like a broken record, repeating the same three words, and I had already used them!

I smiled at the audience then turned to Andrew Olle, who was master of ceremonies for the evening. It was Andrew's wonderful interview in 1990 that made James decide to ask me to write the book, he was MC at the launch of the book in Sydney in 1992, and now in June 1993 he was handing me the Book of the Year award.

So I gave him the best smile I could muster, all the while having a raging argument with my brain. But still I was faced with a blank wall.

My eyes fell on the beautiful red leather-bound version of my book I had been handed when I stepped on stage and had been clutching to my chest ever since. In a reflex action I held up the book and the words started to tumble out of my mouth. 'This book has changed my life,' came the emotional beginning, then I was back on track. I told the story of James making an appointment with me for the next day after the interview. He had arrived at my hotel while I was rushing across town to his office, overawed at the prospect of speaking to a publisher.

But the part of the speech the audience enjoyed most was when I spoke of arriving at the Pan Macmillan offices on a Saturday and being let in by the cleaning woman. We then sat down to cup of tea and I asked her to give me a rundown on James.

I'm not sure what else I talked about, something followed, then I thanked everyone.

After I finished I worried about having stood onstage for such a length of time saying nothing. Jeannine assured me it was all of ten seconds before I gathered myself, but to me it seemed more like ten minutes.

What a day! I had journeyed from the pits of despair when I heard about the book being peddled discrediting *From Strength to Strength* to standing before the people of the book industry receiving an award for the book.

The next day I was back at the book fair signing books and still on a major high, when a beaming James came up to me and said there were no takers for the discrediting book. The agent had done the rounds of the publishers, except Pan Macmillan, and no-one was interested! With the threat over, I hit an even greater high.

Following the award, *From Strength to Strength* went to number-one position on the bestseller lists—higher than my current book—and I went back to Bullo floating on a cloud.

While I was receiving the award in Sydney, Marlee was in the yards drafting cattle. She had had the usual cuts and bruises from handling cattle all year, but one day she opened the drafting gate to let a cow into the round yard, but as she pushed the gate closed a very stroppy bull also tried to charge through the gate. Marlee closed the gate quickly to block him and his horn squashed her thumb up against the top steel rail of the gate. As you can imagine, it was excruciatingly painful—the finger split open, the nail went black and the finger resembled a light bulb. The doctor said she would definitely lose the nail, was lucky not to lose the top of her finger. It healed remarkably well and a perfect nail grew in place of the horrible black mess that fell off a few weeks later. Only a slight scar on the inside of the thumb remained.

July was busy, with mustering, a TV crew filming a segment for *11 a.m.* and Franz's mum and dad, Mama and Papa Ranacher, arriving from Austria. They were very excited about coming to the outback of Australia—well, Marlee and I had to rely on Franz for this information, because his parents didn't speak English. Before their arrival we madly learnt German, which we knew would only help a bit as they spoke the Austrian dialect, and Franz's parents took English lessons.

Once they arrived we were able to exchange a few words but the weeks ahead were mainly filled with constant charades as we tried to get across our message. Whenever Franz arrived back at the house we would get him to translate our conversations and both sides would collapse into peals of laughter. I had one twenty-minute conversation with Papa and didn't have a clue what it was about. I think he was in the same boat!

They are wonderful people and everyone enjoyed every minute of their visit. If someone asked me to describe the visit in one word, I would have to say, 'laughter'.

We also had another overseas visitor staying with us at this time. At a conference on New Zealand's South Island a man had come up to me and told me he built roads. He had read in my book what trouble we had with our road over the mountains. He said that building roads over mountains was his everyday trade and was sure he could help us. Having driven around the South Island I knew exactly what he meant, there were roads hanging off the sides of mountains! I explained the job was very extensive and the problem was we didn't have the millions required to hire people to do the work. I thanked him very much for his concern and went on signing books.

I should have realised that a roadbuilder from the South Island wouldn't give up that easily. A week or so after I came home from my tour he was on the phone. He was planning a holiday to Australia and would like to come to Bullo to look at our road to see if there was anything he could do to help.

So here he was. Over the years since, Bill Ward's help has been much more than just on the road, and he has become a wonderful friend. To give one example, he once lent us his top mechanic for six weeks when we had urgent repair work and couldn't find a mechanic with heavy machinery experience.

I had to leave Bill and Mama and Papa Ranacher in Marlee and Jacqui's capable hands, because I was off again on the conference circuit. Well, first it was a fundraiser for the Peter Pan Society, then onto a conference for Tupperware at Darling Harbour for about 1,400 people. The *11 a.m.* crew wanted to film me at a conference, to contrast with the shots on the station and what a conference this was!

This was the yearly awards day for sales at all those Tupperware parties. I had no idea they were still going on! When I went back to the Outback in 1970 after returning from America, Tupperware parties were quite the thing. Here it was twenty-three years later and they were still going strong. Just one look at these 1,400 dedicated women and you'd know why. Can you imagine how the dust would fly if we put them into Canberra to spring clean?

In my speeches I can always manage to link the company I am speaking for to a story about the Outback. Sometimes this has been hard, but a story always seems to surface. But this looked like it was going to be the first time I couldn't find a story. For weeks I had been trying to think of a story that tied Tupperware into my life in the Outback, and right up until I walked on stage to speak, I couldn't think of one.

Then as I was being introduced, I looked at the Tupperware products on the prize table in front of me and the story came to me, as if it happened only yesterday. It had actually happened way back in 1965, on one of my few journeys to the front gate that year.

I would not drive up or down our first jump-up (a very steep, sharply rising road, up a cliff face) because it was so dangerously steep. The steep grade and the dreadful condition of all our vehicles back in the early days was a lethal mixture. If the brakes failed, the road was so narrow and winding there was nowhere to go but over the cliff, backwards. I would wait at the bottom of the jump-up with the girls while Charlie roared safely to the top of the pass, then the girls and I would walk to the top.

One day, Charlie was at the last steep section of the climb and he changed gears quickly to get more power out of the old engine and he stalled. He restarted the utility and took off with a mighty lurch. It was so violent he dislodged the picnic basket along with quite a few other items out of the back. I watched as various things crashed and tumbled down the road towards me or over the cliff face.

When I reached the scene most of the gear had been picked up, and Charlie looked at me with his charming sorry expression, 'Not much of the picnic set survived, we will have to drink water out of our hats. Most of the cups and plates are smashed. But this survived.'

He handed me the Tupperware container with the sandwiches for lunch safely inside. Mum had packed this handy container in my suitcase on my first journey into the Outback, and I had used it for so many things. It was now covered in dust and quite badly scratched having tumbled down the rocky road, but it hadn't broken open and the sandwiches were in A-1 condition. This story was enthusiastically received. I then retired to the foyer to sign books.

The announcement for the start of the next session caused a surge towards me. Eager women wanting everything from books to hats to conference ribbons signed, pinning me against the wall in the process. I now know what it feels like to be mobbed! An orderly, very dignified mobbing, but a mobbing nevertheless.

I signed furiously until the final call then the women noisily withdrew into the auditorium and the foyer fell quiet. The reporter from *11 a.m.* was amazed, associating this type of behaviour with rock stars and the young, and asked me if this happened all the time.

'Nope, that's my first mobbing,' I replied.

I dropped by my publishers' offices, to say hello and discuss plans for the rest of the year. James had another of those great grins he gets when something good has happened.

'What?' was my only word. I knew it would come

out in a rush in the next two seconds, that was James! He handed me a letter which said I had been awarded (take a deep breath, this is a long title) The Angus & Robertson Bookworld Australian Author Non-Fiction Literary Medal for 1994. Whew!

James proudly handed me a large picture frame about two-and-a-half feet tall and there in the middle, amongst lots of writing, nestling in satin, was a gold medal. I headed for home with my picture frame under my arm.

It was soon back to cattle musters, accounts, office work, tourists, writing, and another interesting event. All kinds of interesting and strange events were becoming the norm in my life of late. On the 30th July a team of thirteen men were arriving to set up camp on Bullo— on the front lawn to be precise. They hoped to locate the lost anchors of the exploration ship, the *Beagle*, out of the Victoria River's muddy depths.

This was the second time this ship had brought interesting people to our doorstep. Years earlier I had had a visit from the managing director of a Queensland-based oil company. He was also a historian and had read in the log of the *Beagle* that the longboat rowed up the Bullo River as far as an oil slick. So he wanted to send a drilling team to Bullo to find the source of the oil slick. They drilled down to depths of one mile, but found nothing favourable in the core samples to indicate oil. The geologist left me a souvenir piece of the core, supposedly many millions of years old.

Now we had a team consisting of all manner of

professionals on an *Australian Geographic* expedition. With very modern technology at their disposal, this team, together with the enthusiastic Dick Smith, was confident they would find the anchors.

Marlee and I knew nothing about the ability of the very impressive machines we saw unloaded, but we did know our area, and especially the mud in the Victoria and Bullo rivers. If the anchors had been there for over a hundred years, we would bet anything they would stay for the rest of time! A forty-five foot fishing barge once got stuck on the mud in the Bullo River and even though it took a few years, the barge slowly slipped out of sight into the seemingly bottomless mud.

I suppose you could call our mud slow-motion quick-sand. We just call it suction mud. Once you're in it, it's quite a problem getting out, and if you were silly enough to stand around for an hour or so, you too would disappear.

It once took several hours just to dig out the four legs of a horse. Anything bigger than a horse's hoof would take days. Something large could take months. And this does not take into account the tide that turns the mud into syrup.

We told these stories to Dick Smith when he dropped by one day in the middle of 1993 in his Sikorsky helicopter. He and his wife Pip were off to England on one of his around-the-world trips. This is when we met Jim Hazelton who was being dropped off in Indonesia to pick up an aircraft.

They all sat in the living room at Bullo and listened politely to our terrible tales of mud. When we had

Danielle and Martin cutting their wedding cake.

Club Med II, where I was guest speaker on the cruise.

Franz and his mum, resting while working in the cattle yards.

The bogged fuel truck that Marlee and Franz had to rescue.

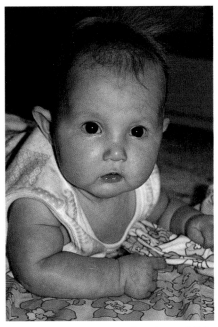

Natalie Clair Jennings, first-born child to Danielle and Martin.

Natalie with her little brother John.

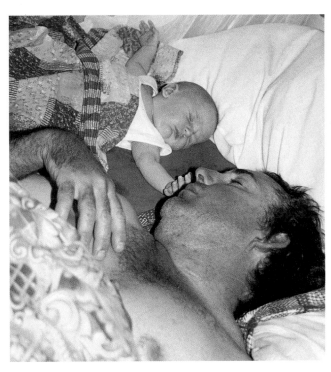

Baby John with Dad.

One of the many conferences at Darling Harbour.

Marlee with me in San Francisco, signing books.

The view from my window in the Ranacher home,
where I was finishing *Some of My Friends Have Tails*.

Marlee, Franz and me at Gold Deck skiing resort in Austria.

Papa Ranacher working in the 400-year-old workshop.
When I stepped into this room I felt I was in Santa's workshop.

Marlee at Katherine Show with Bazza, our Bazadaise bull, who won first prize.

Aunty Sue, trying to
teach me to pose, at her
place in Caloundra.

Signing books on tour for
Some of My Friends Have Tails.

finished the lengthy recital, Dick asked if we would like to go for a fly in the Sikorsky over Holdfast Reach, where the anchors were cut loose. It was clear that mud or no mud, he intended to find the anchors. So we stopped talking and went for a ride.

Being used to mustering helicopters, we were a little in awe of our surroundings. This was like sitting in the backseat of a Rolls. True, it was outfitted especially for a trip around the world, but it was a very special machine, equipped with a fax machine and nose and rear cameras with an in-house television screen to show you exactly what the camera was viewing. The electronics were staggering to people from the middle of nowhere. We are still marvelling over the remote control to our television! But if you stop and remember the chopper belonged to Dick Smith, the electronics couldn't be anything else but state of the art.

After a great flight they deposited us back on the front lawn, Dick assuring us before he departed that a team would be back with him in 1994. We then watched the big machine glide effortlessly off in the direction of Darwin.

There is a wonderful account of their *Beagle* adventure in the April 1995 issue of *Australian Geographic*.

According to this article, the team had to wait until they were back in Sydney before they could read the findings. Apparently there are three hot spots that could represent the two anchors and the fifty metres or so of chain that also went down. So they are fairly certain where the anchors are, they just have to bring them up from their resting place.

83

Getting to know Dick Smith in the short time he was here, I have no doubt he will be back. But as determined as he is, he will face a mighty challenge. He might know the location of the anchors but getting them out of the mud will not be easy. One of these anchors, the main or bow which is 3.4 metres high, presents major problems. To raise something this size the mud would have to be cleared and kept away while the anchor was being brought to the surface. The *Australian Geographic* report says the anchors are in ten metres of water, but no-one knows the depth of the mud. My guess is there are about another twenty metres of mud.

I don't know what kind of machine could move so much mud under ten metres of water and keep it out of the way. Perhaps a few giant dredges. The biggest problem that will be faced is that the moment you dig a hole it vanishes. To get the anchors out would cost a fortune and even then, I'll bet on the mud! But the impossible does happen on a regular basis.

A few weeks later after I had attended conferences on Hamilton Island and in New Zealand, and spent time with Sue and Ralph in Caloundra, I was back home when a charming man turned up in a big flashy plane with a bunch of orchids and a meal from an exclusive restaurant. He had read my book and was fascinated by my Marlee. He thought she would be great for his son, whom he indicated needed to be brought into line and he was sure Marlee was the one to do this. He was most disappointed to find she was married as he had only read the first book. We had a lovely lunch, however, then he boarded his plane and disappeared out of our lives. As I said, strange things happen to me on a regular basis.

By this time I had received lots of letters and phone calls about the audiotape of *From Strength to Strength* which had been on the market since April. (I do get the chance to open and read letters, I just don't get the time to answer them.) There was no tour for the tape, but from all reports it was selling well, and it had been on the shortlist for the audiotape of the year. Well, it did have a lucky launch date—it went onto the market on Marlee's birthday!

One woman had been listening to the tape while on a long country drive. When she got to the part where Marlee's Charlie died she was sobbing uncontrollably and couldn't see the road. So she pulled over to the side of the road, rested her head on the steering wheel, and had a good cry.

A police patrol car pulled over and the officer asked if she was OK. In between sobs she managed to say she was all right, but had just been listening to the tape of a book by Sara Henderson. Whereupon the policeman interrupted her and said, 'Oh struth! My wife is reading that book, I know all about it! One minute she is bawling her eyes out, next minute she falls out of bed laughing! I'll be bloody glad when she finishes it and she's back to normal again!'

Another woman was listening to the tape on a walkman going to work in the train. She stopped when she realised she was the entertainment every morning as the other passengers watched her laugh and cry and go through the whole gamut of emotions. Many people also came up to her on the platform and asked the name of the tape. Another woman got a similar reaction on a plane when people turned around and looked down the aisle each time she burst into uncontrollable laughter or sobbing.

The biggest disaster in our lives, house-wise, occurred on the 12th August. Jacqui, our wonderful housekeeper, decided to go back to civilisation, leaving the day after the *Australian Geographic* team departed. In the following weeks while I was away Marlee had to juggle the house, meals, guests and mustering with Franz as her assistant. We had a long line of would-be cooks. But after Jacqui, no-one was up to the standard to which we had become accustomed! The shock was a major one, after such a long stretch of order and neatness and good meals.

Marlee had a difficult time rushing from the cattle yards to the kitchen to cook for incoming guests, then back to the yards to draft cattle. We kept hoping, and I did some heavy praying, for someone reasonable to magically appear. No such luck, in fact for the fifteen months following Jacqui's departure, according to the tax records we went through eleven cooks, trying to find her prayed-for replacement.

Marlee had to carry the full brunt of this situation, with me away almost full-time until December. It was a very hard time for her, but she made it through to the end of the tourist period and we certainly didn't book in any extra guests for the rest of the year. The poor old house slowly slipped backwards, and gone was our sparkling, orderly homestead. It was clean and tidy, but only just, as staff came and left every few weeks with monotonous regularity.

These added pressures, along with my diary from hell, had my life spinning out of control again. The workload for the rest of the year had me worried, and I was fearful of slipping back towards the black hole again.

My looming schedule for the following few months was overwhelming. From the 4th of August to the 25th October I would have exactly eight days at home!

CHAPTER 6

September 1994–
December 1994

*A*fter a short writing break at home I flew to Sydney for a dinner speech, then rushed to the airport to catch a late flight to Melbourne and drove to Gippsland to speak at a breakfast gathering the next morning. I returned to Melbourne to speak at a dinner and flew to Sydney the next morning for my following engagement.

My next conference was one with a difference. This one was in San Francisco. And what I was really looking forward to was that Marlee was meeting me in Sydney and coming with me. The company holding the conference had special travel arrangements and said I could bring someone with me. It was now September, and there was a big enough break in between guests for Marlee to take a well-earned rest, so she was pretty excited about going off to San Francisco for seven days. For me, it was also a much-needed break, and to not be travelling alone for once was simply wonderful!

We had a day together in Sydney before we left and I caught up with all the station news. It seemed cupid had been busy again and we had another love match on Bullo. This was getting to be an annual event. One romance every year for four years running was pretty amazing! I don't think dating agencies get that percentage! I keep saying it must be something in the water, but I drink a lot of water and nothing has happened to me yet! I guess I must be either immune to this love bug or that old bastard Charlie is up to his old tricks again!

On Marlee's way through Darwin she had made a few last-minute arrangements for the latest wedding; nice little touches like a small bouquet of flowers and a horse and carriage to take the lovebirds to the registry office. A wedding cake had been made at Bullo and iced by the other girls there and Marlee took it to Darwin and added some finishing touches. Franz and Marlee were the witnesses for the ceremony and the cake was presented to the newlyweds in the registry office. And so another Bullo River love knot was tied and all in the few hours before Marlee's flight to Sydney. Our long flight to San Francisco passed with us catching up on plans for the next few months and mapping out the future of the station. In between this and dozing, I was writing notes for my next book.

We stayed in a new hotel so massive, it had four floors of conference rooms alone. The hotel was so big it was frightening. When we finally found our room there was a two-page list of instructions attached to the back of the door telling us the dangers of being in San Francisco!

Rules like not to answer your door to anyone, and double locking your door after entering the room. The rule of having to check with reception before opening your door if there was a fire had me seriously thinking that maybe we should get on the next plane home!

We read in the information folder that when all the guest and conference rooms were full, added to hotel staff of a few thousand, there would be ten thousand people in the building. I didn't sleep much, visualising how all those people could get out of the hotel, having to check with reception first!

The first morning I was a handed a business card by a conference manager of a reporter who wanted to interview me for the local paper. Marlee and I went along and met the reporter in the foyer, and he immediately complained it was too noisy to interview me on tape, and suggested we go up to our room where it would be quiet. Immediately all the rules on the back of the door flashed before my eyes and I said no! It took a good few minutes to get through to him he was not going to get into our room, under any circumstances. He finally settled for an appointment in the foyer after lunch.

Just before I left the room for the interview there was a phone call from reception. Our intrepid reporter had told them he had an appointment with me and could they give him our room number. He was definitely persistent, but I had had enough of his games, so said no and told them to get security to check him out.

He did a bunk before security reached reception and no-one saw him again.

Marlee had not been well for a few days during this

holiday and so I was back on the phone to reception. I was given the telephone number of what they called their 'house doctor'. I told him Marlee's symptoms and asked if he could come and see her. He told me what that would cost, and after picking the phone up off the floor, I said maybe I could get Marlee into a cab to come and see him. He asked me if she had health insurance then suggested we could meet him at the hospital. He said he would probably have to operate straight away.

I wasn't too impressed with a doctor who didn't even want to examine a patient before he decided to operate and with his major concern being whether we had health insurance so I slammed the phone down and called our doctor in Australia. After I pushed Marlee many times in the stomach area, following his instructions, he said it sounded like a slight attack of appendicitis. She was to rest, and as the attack didn't seem severe and there was no pain in her side as yet, it might pass. If she didn't improve after twenty-four hours and pain developed we were to find another doctor, one less gung-ho than our 'house doctor'.

When faced with these alarming facts, I think Marlee willed herself better. She lay in bed feeling miserable with me watching her every breath, and asking her how she felt every hour. We saw a wide variety of American television, and I did a lot of work on my manuscript, with one eye always on Marlee. She told me later, she improved after a day and a half just to stop me asking the question, 'How do you feel now?'

San Francisco had changed greatly since the last time I was there, many years before, and was now very commercialised. I liked the old San Fran better, but who can stop progress?

We heaved a deep sigh of relief as we stepped on board our Qantas flight. This was not our kind of country and we were keen to get back to the bush, and Australia, where we had some idea of the system. We flew into Sydney and had a day together before Marlee boarded a plane for Darwin and I continued on the conference trail.

I was off to Perth this time and back to Sydney the same night on the red-eye flight to speak the next day. Then it was onto Canberra late that night for a director's meeting early the next morning. The following day I flew to Brisbane and had two days off in Caloundra to write and catch up on messages and business. The next round of travel was much shorter with only one speech, a book signing in a downtown bookstore in Adelaide and home the next day! I made it back to Bullo on the 25th September. I also had a birthday somewhere in the middle of all that. I had forgotten, but the girls remembered; Marlee and Danielle sent me lovely flowers and chocolates.

I was home for three days, but needed all that time to pack my clothes for the next round of travelling. It was a rather long journey this time—all of October. I started with the New Zealand Women's Book Festival. So I found myself touring around New Zealand for the second time that year.

October was a perfect example of how I had slipped

back into overbooking my every moment. When an engagement fitted nicely into a timeslot, was convenient and I was in the same city or nearby, I would think, 'Yes, I can do that easily.'

After spending the 1st to the 9th touring New Zealand, I flew to Sydney for a fundraising luncheon on the 11th, conducted business the next two days, flew to Brisbane for a conference on the 14th, spent the 15th and 16th writing in Caloundra then flew to Melbourne to speak on the 18th. Conferences on the Gold Coast, in Brisbane, and Sydney followed and I was back home on the 23rd. I had four days at home for writing full-time and doing only the emergency office work. I had another conference in Brisbane on the 28th then I could spend a whole ten days at home before my next engagement.

My life was not my own again and I had to fall back on the only method of survival: 'No, sorry I am not available.'

I was determined that after the last engagement on the 30th November, I was going home and not moving out of Bullo for the whole of December. Except, of course, for the yearly Christmas shopping trip to Darwin with Marlee. But before I could do that I still had four conferences, a fundraiser and two days of director's meetings to attend, all in different cities.

Back at Bullo there was so much unopened mail from readers it now had its own room! I was also only a quarter of the way through writing my next book which had to be finished by the following March. So December would have to see some serious writing. To achieve this

93

I said no to so many last-minute requests for December functions, I lost count. But I had to be tough as one glance at 1995 told me it was already well and truly overbooked.

The undoubted highlight of November was when Danielle gave birth to a beautiful baby girl on the 9th. Natalie Clair Jennings was born at the Mount Isa Base Hospital at 10.18 a.m., weighing in at 4.08 kilos. And of course, even though I only had four engagements that month, she arrived as I was on my way to a conference on Hamilton Island.

I hadn't made it to Cloncurry once during Danielle's pregnancy and she was so busy helping Martin with their ever-expanding cement company she couldn't come home to Bullo or meet me in any city on my travels in Queensland for a break.

When I finally made it to Cloncurry I took care of my little granddaughter while Danielle rushed off every morning with Martin to yet another urgent job. Just when I was down to the last bottle of milk Danielle would rush in the door, express more milk into bottles, kiss Natalie and disappear again. My visit was a bit like one of my book tours—looking after a baby again after twenty-four years and keeping up with Danielle and Martin's schedule was totally exhausting!

The other remarkable event in November was that Mrs Henderson, Charlie's mother, turned 104!

There was bad weather around the world, with floods in Italy and France, violent storms in Victoria and snow in Tasmania. It was reasonable to assume the north wouldn't get off scot-free. And we didn't. The fuel truck left Kununurra on a five-hour trip to the homestead. During that time we had a violent storm which dumped a lot of rain on the road out in the mountain area of our road. At the beginning of the rainy season the road can usually take many inches of rain before it is even wet, let alone boggy. But the gravel topping is wearing thin and a large section chopped up by the roadtrains carting the cattle out had turned one part into a deep bog. This section was covered by a thin layer of gravel neatly packed down by the heavy rain and so looked just the same as the rest of the smooth gravel road. The driver couldn't see anything wrong with the road and it was only when he was halfway across the section that the big rig just started to sink. There was nothing he could do except sit and watch the whole rig behind him sink slowly down to the axles. The prime-mover went down so far into the mud he had to climb up to get out the window!

The driver called his depot on the two-way radio and they called us with the good news!

The depot omitted to mention the rig was bogged down to the axles so when Marlee and Franz arrived on the scene to pull him out with the grader and chains and other equipment, they took one look at the semi and it was back to the workshop, twenty-two miles back down the road, to get the frontend loader and the D8 bulldozer. This was going to be something to move.

95

Our bank manager was visiting and came to see if he could help in any way. When he wanted to know if Marlee was going to push the rig out, she knew this was his first semi bog, or indeed his first anything bog. He learned a lot that day about removing a trailer and prime-mover loaded with 22,000 litres of fuel in bulk containers and twenty-four two-hundred-litre drums from a sea of mud. He now knows you don't push, you pull.

It took every ounce of the D8's horsepower to move the rig. In fact Marlee had to pull it out backwards (she is the expert with the bulldozer), because the cab was so far down in the mud and the road was too boggy at the front end of the rig to get any real pulling power. The chains broke many times as she had to repeatedly jerk the rig to get it moving. The pull was over a fair distance because the ground behind the semi was also boggy and Marlee didn't want the dozer to end up in the bog along with the semi. After many hours, five long towing chains had become twenty-eight short towing chains, but the rig was finally standing on the hard gravel section of the road, looking very sorry for itself. It was covered in thick mud almost to the top of the cabin and the tankers on the trailer were one big blob. The fuel truck finally delivered the fuel to the homestead and on his way home, the driver avoided the mega bog hole he had created.

December was not all time off. We had Bernie O'Kane, our Bazadaise breeder, Dave Morris the vet and a team of Bernie's friends from Cobram, Victoria staying for a

week or so to transplant embryos, pure Bazadaise fertil-
ised eggs, into some of our cows, making them surrogate
mothers. We also had two hundred and fifty cows to
artificially inseminate. This was part of our introduction
of the French Bazadaise blood into our herd—we aptly
named this new Brahman–Bazadaise cross Bullion. Our
aim in bringing this new breed into the North was for
faster growth rate in our herd, and to turn off three-
hundred-kilogram offsprings the same year of weaning.
This week was a busy one with Bernie and his mob at
the homestead, but I left them in the capable hands of
Marlee and Franz and worked day and night on the
manuscript, only appearing for meals. I wish I could
have spent more time with them down in the yards, but
my deadline for the book kept me at my desk.

After a busy time of ploughing and cattle work at the
beginning of the month, December quietened down.
We had a small group of people for Christmas and
enjoyed the peace and the short break. As short as my
rest was, I took anything I could get. 1995 was looking
decidedly busy, with the manuscript to be handed in by
March, a book tour of England and then meeting up
afterwards with Marlee and Franz in Austria for what I
hoped would be some sort of holiday. It was then onto
a book tour of South Africa. And before I left for overseas I had to do a television commercial.

The last few days of December were spent getting the
house ready for the television crew arriving on the 1st
January. There were thirteen people coming so we had

to find somewhere for them all to sleep. Two girls were helping in the house and Marlee would be cooking for our staff and the television crew—a total of twenty people. I was to be assistant cook, but we didn't hold much hope that I would have any spare time away from the camera, except for a few hours here and there.

The two girls working in the house left after just three days of getting ready. I think their departing words were, 'We weren't hired to be slaves!'

The next two girls we hired didn't think cleaning the house, making beds and preparing guest rooms was being a slave. They were very thankful to have a job. They had seen our notice on the job board at the backpacker hostel in Darwin. They hadn't been able to get a job anywhere in Darwin and were down to their last dollar. Not knowing where your next meal is coming from tends to give you the right attitude in a job, and they were a delight to have around.

I fell asleep in front of the television on New Year's Eve, completely exhausted from bedmaking, dusting and helping Marlee cook meals for freezing in case there were problems in the following week and Marlee had to be something other than the cook.

I woke up at 11.30 p.m. to find I was alone in the living room—everyone had gone to bed, too tired to wait for the New Year. It was so close to midnight I decided to stay up and welcome the New Year. I took a cold beer out of the chiller and reclined in a deckchair out on the lawn, staring at the beautiful stars in the crystal-clear sky, and reminiscing about the year just about to end.

Daisy, our milking cow, wandered over to investigate the deckchair and the dogs were on alert immediately. I told them to hush and to leave her alone. They settled again and Daisy continued to waddle by, looking all the world like a cartoon character. She was in the garden because she was close to giving birth and we were keeping an eye on her. She seemed restless and looked like a balloon ready to burst and I knew we would see her baby in the next few days. Pumpkin, our other milking cow, had beaten her by about a week—she'd had her calf just before Christmas.

I raised my glass to Charlie on the hill as I thought about the year gone, told him to keep helping us and wandered off to bed knowing the year ahead was going to be a challenge, once again. And it was going to start at a blistering pace on the very first day with the filming of a television commercial.

As I walked to my bedroom, the dogs strolling quietly behind me, a big sigh escaped from my lips, making them stop and look at me enquiringly. I smiled at their loving faces and said, 'Well, that's another year over. What do you think this new year will bring us?'

They wagged their short stumpy tails vigorously. I decided that was a good sign and went happily to bed.

During the early hours of the morning I woke to find Daisy standing right outside my open bedroom window, lovingly licking a tiny little baby calf standing very unsteadily on long, wobbly legs. I drifted back to sleep smiling.

CHAPTER 7

January 1995–
March 1995

There was no sleeping in or resting on New Year's Day, it was up at the crack of dawn as we had thirteen visitors arriving for afternoon tea! The television crew was landing in Darwin around lunchtime and by the time they packed themselves into a few charter planes and headed down to Bullo, it would be late afternoon. So we had most of the day to finish our preparation and as usual we needed every minute.

I was making the first of the Breastscreen commercials for the Department of Health. The campaign, we hoped, would make people aware of the importance of having a regular mammogram.

About the middle of 1994 I had received a fax from the Department of Health asking me if I would consider being the spokeswoman for a new breast cancer awareness campaign. I asked why me, and was told it was the result of a survey of three thousand women. The women were given the names of ten well-known women and asked to pick the woman they were most likely to listen to. They ended up with my name. So I have my readers to thank, once again, for giving me the opportunity to be part of such a wonderful and worthwhile campaign.

I recently signed a new contract that goes into 1999, so it looks like I will be telling you this important message for a little while longer!

I initially suggested someone who had fought breast cancer and won would be a better choice. But the answer was no, they were trying to get women to have an X-ray to prevent cancer, so they needed someone the women would listen to, and someone, like them, who did not have breast cancer.

I said there was no breast cancer in my family, so I was certainly safe. Then I was quoted a statistic which I found hard to believe—in nine out of ten cases of breast cancer diagnosed, there is no history of breast cancer in the family. This really stunned me as here I was going along thinking whenever I saw anything about breast cancer, 'Well, that doesn't concern me, no-one in my family has had this dreadful disease.'

If I didn't know this crucial statistic about breast cancer and I was looking after people's health on the station, how many other women had the same thought in their heads? This was the reason I decided to do the commercial. Even though I was trying to slow this public life of mine down, there are some things I believe must be done, regardless.

I have been unofficially in charge of the health of all the people on the station since I first arrived. I am sure

101

my children grew up thinking I was a doctor. One actually told someone on the phone one morning, 'Mummy is in surgery, could you call back later,' when I was taking stitches out of a stockman's wound.

Apart from the fact I have always been interested in medicine, the entire health of everyone on a cattle station just seems to be the responsibility of the missus. Whether she likes this job, or knows anything about medicine, seems to be beside the point.

When the arrangements to shoot the commercial began, they asked if the crew could come to the station in January to do the shoot. I explained a few of the trials of trying to do anything in January in the Outback. The heat, for a start, would cause all sorts of trouble for all of them—we had had many camera crews over the years trying to capture the beauty of the North in the wet and on some occasions the film had melted in the camera. The bugs swarm in the thousands so I told them there was no way they could do any filming inside under lights—the last time that was tried during the wet within minutes so many bugs had fallen onto a light they covered the bulb and the heat of the high-voltage bulb set them on fire.

After I'd told them just a few of the problems, they rang back and said January was the only time they could get to Bullo which would coincide with me being there.

The first day of shooting nearly finished everyone off. A commercial is not shot as you see it on screen— a bit's shot here, a piece there, and nothing seems to make any sense. But the shooting follows a precise plan and somehow it all jells together and, miraculously, they come up with a commercial. The idea was to get the difficult shots over with first, so the schedule for the first day was to shoot at the front gate, fifty miles away. The logistics of the front-gate shoot were incredible, so it was suggested initially that we make a mock-up front gate at the homestead. However it was decided that too many people had seen the front gate in pictures in my books, so we would have to use the real McCoy.

By the time the people, gear and equipment were packed into vehicles, and the journey down our road over the mountain ranges was completed, we arrived at the gate at midday. It was blisteringly hot as the heat bounced off the sandstone ridges of the Pinkerton Range, and there are very few trees for shade. Most of the crew had brought flasks with them which held about one litre of water. These were emptied on the trip along the road, so when we arrived there was a rush on the cool-drink esky Marlee had packed. This supply also ran out, as it was just too hot to be out. I was used to this heat but certainly didn't go out in the sun at midday. These people were from the South, were dressed in shorts and sleeveless tops, and doing their best to stay out of the sun, while trying to shoot a commercial.

In one of the takes, I had to lean on the top rail of the front gate, my arms folded casually, with the Bullo River sign clearly showing underneath. The steel was so hot it burnt me through my shirtsleeves.

By the time the shot was set up to the director's satisfaction the cameras had been in the sun for too long and were too hot. So cameras had to be kept in the shade, and film in an esky. The cameras were lugged back and forth from the shade of a tree 150 feet away when the shot was ready, then back after the shot was finished.

A weary group of very sunburned people dragged themselves back into the homestead that night looking so beat Marlee and I didn't have the heart to say we told you so.

It was rush hour in the swimming pool, there were long showers, and a lot of lotion and sunburn cream was smeared on. Then after a good meal everyone disappeared to bed, very early, thankful for one thing, at least they didn't have to go to the front gate again. They weren't the only ones glad about that, I can tell you!

The next day was a breeze in comparison—just around the homestead taking shots with my beloved horse Boots. He was his usual self, stealing the show in all the takes.

The final shot for the day was a silhouette shot of Boots and me standing against the red sunset. It came out really well in the finished commercial. However there were a few hiccups during filming. I had lent my new riding boots to one of the staff the season before and they hadn't been returned, so I had to borrow Franz's boots which were a size twelve! I didn't have to walk, which was fortunate but while I was concentrating on keeping my boots under control, the crew were looking everywhere but at us and delaying the shot. Finally one of the girls said, 'Boots is being indiscreet.'

There he was in silhouette with all his stallion's assets on full display. I told them the problem was easily

solved. A few tickles on his tummy and everything disappeared—everyone was impressed.

Because we had been filming only at sunrise and
sunset, and doing the inside shots during the day to
escape the bugs, we began to run out of time. So it was
back to filming during the day.

The following day was the most tiring day I had experienced for a long time. The take was the now famous
'then you bloody well should' swearing commercial.

I get so many letters that start, 'Dear Sara, I bloody
well have!' And I am so glad this turned out to be the
best commercial because it took blood, sweat, tears and
a lot of swearing to get it done.

After the director had given me instructions for the
commercial, I stared at him, thinking he was joking. I had
to remember a lengthy speech—I couldn't change a word
because it had all been vetted by the legal department—
and hit a bump when the script required, looking cool,
comfortable and relaxed! I walked towards the Toyota
with one thought on my mind—the man is mad!

Thinking this was going to be one right royal stuff-
up, I learnt there was more! The cameraman—who
deserves the Victoria Cross—had to hang out the
passenger-side door on ropes in order to get the camera
far enough away to film me driving. He had to keep the
camera steady, so I had to drive so he wouldn't lose his
balance, at the same time as watching for trees along the
edge of the road so as not to wrap him around one.
Also, the shot had to be done as quickly as possible
because the camera was heavy and it was around thirty-
eight degrees in the shade.

Oh well, here goes, I thought, it has got to be done so you'd better get to and do it! Although how well, I had lots of doubts about at this point.

While the cameraman was being tied into position, I was learning my lines and mopping perspiration from my face. There were no make-up artists running around dabbing every time a drop of sweat appeared, in fact there were no make-up artists at all. Whatever make-up I had put on that morning had long since gone with the constant mopping of sweat, so I was what you might call 'natural'.

The cameraman was ready, hanging out the door on metre-long ropes balancing a hefty camera, the director called 'Ready' and I started the engine. I went up through the gears carefully so as not to jerk the camera-man off balance, and tried to look into the camera as if I didn't have a care in the world. I kept glancing at the road so I didn't go bush, and watched the trees on the passenger side so we didn't lose the cameraman. I hit a bump where the script demanded and finished with a convincing, 'then you bloody well should!' I brought the Toyota to a halt under the shade of a tree, then waited for the results.

When you finish a take, I had learned by now, that was not the end of things by a long way. First you look at the director who usually looks like he has just had his teeth pulled without anaesthetic. Then after a few minutes you get a decision—sometimes favourable, sometimes not. Then your eyes travel to the cameraman whose response is more businesslike, either a 'Yes' or an 'I'd like to do it again'. In this situation I didn't think our cameraman would be saying the latter too often! Then you look at the sound man to see if anyone spoke during the recording and spoilt the tape. Lastly, the client has to be pleased with the results, seeing they are the ones paying, and the advertising agency has to put in their two bits.

The results this time were not good. The director thought we could do better and gave me a few tips on my delivery. The cameraman wanted to try another lens—so it obviously didn't faze him hanging out in midair and relying on me not to sideswipe him on a tree! The sound man just said, 'Sorry no good' as the noise of the engine as I moved up the gears was so loud it ruined the whole take, and the client chipped in that I had said 'will' instead of 'can' and that was a legal no-no.

I said a few choice four-letter words under my breath, got back into the Toyota, ran through my lines, wiped the sweat now pouring down my face, and backed up to the starting line. This time I had to get through the gears in record time before I started to speak. I did some swift gear changes that would have impressed Marlee, managed to not wrap the cameraman around a tree, hit the bump, then completely forgot my lines. I backed up to the starting line disgusted, even swearing on camera, not the words in the script though!

I don't remember how many takes there were before there was a 'Yes' from every department. To me it felt like forever. It was close to fifty degrees in the cabin of the utility and I had visions of me looking like a talking beetroot in the finished commercial.

One of the biggest problems was that I had received various scripts in the mail and had done a good job of memorising those. So good in fact, they kept popping back into my mind every time I was supposed to say the new lines.

The whole crew knew I was a beginner at this game and couldn't do enough to help me. During one of the many pauses while discussions were in progress, I was standing under a tree with the cameraman. I was critical of my performance and apologised for keeping him hanging on ropes. He said not to worry, telling me some professionals do up to twenty takes before they get it right.

I finally whipped through the gears, got all the words right, hit the bump and kept the cameraman in one piece. All of this done looking like I didn't have a care in the world. Only part of a thirty-second commercial had just taken half a day.

The photographer doing the stills for the magazine ads also had his fair share of problems. The camera became so hot at one stage he ended up with a red ring around his right eye where the rim of the viewing lens had burnt his skin.

Apart from some very uncomfortable still shots taken by the photographer in forty-five degree heat, the rest of the takes were a breeze. Well, maybe not a complete breeze. One inside take with me in the saddleroom should have been easy, but caused a considerable amount of trouble. The day had stretched to fifteen hours but we still needed to do one more take to stay on schedule. The harder I tried to get through the few words, the bigger mess I made! The two words 'risk factor' were causing me hell. I just couldn't get my tongue around the phrase with these two words in the middle. Finally, I was handling it so badly, we took a break.

The director offered me a beer, and I immediately said no. If I couldn't get the words out now what would I do after a beer? He assured me it would relax me. As I was past caring by this stage I drank the beer and had a quick bite of food. Then it was back in front of the cameras. I did the take perfectly. The director was delighted and it was thumbs up from every quarter. I sagged with relief and the director said they would have to give me beer every time. He then suggested that since we were on a roll, maybe we could do one more very short shot and wrap it up for the night.

The next take didn't go so smoothly, but we kept at it determined to get it done. The director coached me but I would get one thing right and another thing wrong. He decided we'd have one last go and then leave it. One of the crew jokingly said perhaps I needed another beer.

I took a deep breath and did everything I had been instructed—I got all the words right to satisfy the client, with emotion to make the director happy and clearly to satisfy the sound man. Suddenly the cameraman let out an almighty scream, 'Kill him!'

Silence fell on the scene, all eyes locked on a house guest frozen in the act of handing a can of beer to me on camera. 'What are you doing!' was all I could get out.

He feebly replied that he was only trying to help, someone had said I wanted a beer!

The cameraman was shaking his head and repeating over and over it was a perfect take until a hand with a can of beer came into the last dozen or so frames.

We eventually laughed about turning it into a beer commercial and decided to have one more go. Everything was set when someone asked, 'Where's the beer man?' But our guest had quietly departed to his room. We got a clear take first go, with no beer can!

The commercial was an incredible learning curve for me. It was also very exciting once I got over the camera nerves. Well, I don't think I got over them, I just had them better under control by the end of the shoot.

One thing I had a terrible time conquering was the clapperboard—that little black and white board they put in front of your face at the beginning of each take. I would be ready, with the director's requirements straight, then that thing would snap in front of my face. Everything would disappear and I would stare vacantly at the camera!

I had a few raging arguments with myself trying to deal with this peculiar problem, but I had to admit it was beating me. I explained my problem to the director who simply eliminated the little white board and started with, 'Ready, camera, action!' instead. The change was miraculous.

After sitting in a collapsed heap for most of the day after their departure, it was back to work. I was busy with the office work and packing the business papers I needed to keep running the station while I travelled to four countries. A bigger problem was packing clothes for all seasons for a trip halfway around the world. I was about to embark on book tours of England and Ireland. These would be followed by a holiday in Austria with Marlee and Franz and then another book tour—this time in South Africa.

My first stop was Darwin. There was a good bit of work to be done—papers to be left with the bank and with lawyers and accountants—as I wouldn't be back in Australia until March. I also had a few dentist appointments. Age was telling on my teeth and they were no longer the bright and sparkling teeth of old. I had asked my dentist about whitening teeth. He said he could put a lasting enamel coating over the front of my teeth, which sounded great to me. After I made the appointment for this to be done I had frequent nightmares about my teeth sticking out so far I couldn't speak properly! I called my dentist and voiced my fears and was assured nothing like that would happen. So I went ahead.

It was a time-consuming procedure and a little uncomfortable as my mouth was open for long periods. But there was no pain involved and the results were just amazing. I had my young teeth back! After running my tongue over the new thickness for a few days, I soon forgot the extra layer was there, but was delighted every time I looked in the mirror. Everyone said how well I looked. But no-one picked that it was my rejuvenated teeth that made the difference.

111

My new teeth and I boarded a Qantas flight and were off to London for a ten-day book tour of England. We started the tour on the 12th January, but the book went into the shops on the 13th. There it is again. I wonder if Charlie is sending messages by having very significant events always happen on the 13th? If I meet the man of my dreams on the 13th then I will know he is still in my life. Until then I will go on treating these events as coincidental.

In London I stayed in a delightful old hotel. I have heard of economy of space, but this place took the concept to staggering lengths. With the homestead on Bullo with a quarter of an acre of floor space, I am not what you would call a space economist. So you can imagine how I felt in a room half the size of my dressing room at home. And I had to live there for ten days! The wardrobe was so narrow it wasn't even the width of a coathanger, so everything was hung flat against the wall. Every time I needed something up the back of the wardrobe, everything had to come out and go on the bed. The dressing table was all of ten inches wide. And the bed could only be approached from one side by sliding sideways along the wall. Along with a low ceiling, just barely out of reach, the word cosy came to mind. I like cocoon more.

Having organised my clothes in the small furniture supplied, I had the problem of where to put my suitcase. It had to go somewhere because it took up half the floor space. But alas there was nowhere. So during the day, I put it on the bed and at night we swapped places.

Armed with all my toiletries I headed for the bathroom

door, opened it and backed away, right into the dressing table. The bathroom was smaller than a broom closet. The door swung past the miniature washbasin with two inches to spare, and cleared the toilet seat by about the same amount then slammed into the side of the bath.

I missed a few phone calls when I got wedged between the door and the washbasin and it took a few days before I could slip in and out of the bathroom unimpeded. But after I organised myself, I had to admit it was a nice little room and quite adequate for sleeping in. Once I stopped walking into the walls every time I turned around to move somewhere, I came to enjoy my little hideaway. With the bedroom and bathroom under control, I was ready to attack London.

I didn't realise how much I smiled at people until I stayed in London. I got two reactions to a smile. I was looked at with a cross between alarm and curiosity, or the person would suddenly look in the other direction while watching me carefully out of the corner of one eye. It was the middle of winter, so I suppose after it has been raining for a few months, one doesn't tend to smile much. But after a day of seeing so many serious faces it started to get me down. I did get a daily smile out of the security guard at the BBC, but he was Jamaican. I think it must have something to do with coming from a country where the sun shines regularly. Well, that's my theory.

Seeing I was touring in the middle of winter, it was decided I would do mostly radio broadcasts to all parts of England and Scotland. This was definitely preferable to venturing out into the country and being snowbound for weeks. There were a few daytrips by train to towns close to London, for a luncheon or signing, but then it was back to London at night. I also had a lovely day visiting Bath. Seeing I'm an Agatha Christie fan, I was delighted to see the town and buildings she describes in her books.

So I spent most of my tour inside BBC Broadcast House, receiving a smile from the guard inside the front door, even if I came in three times a day, which I did most days in between television engagements.

I spent most of the time in the regional radio section and the security guard there was a different kettle of fish altogether. This fellow did not utter one word during my entire ten days of comings and goings. I said hello every time I passed through the security point and by about the third day, the silence had become a challenge for me and I was determined to get something out of this fellow, even if it was just the trace of a smile. No such luck. On my last day there wasn't so much as the twitch of an eyebrow when I said, 'Well, you won't see me anymore, I'm off tomorrow. I really enjoyed out little chats.'

The tour finished with me appearing on Irish television on the night of the 21st. When I arrived in the Dublin studio there was a mega drama in progress and unfortunately it involved the host of my scheduled show. Apparently he had been told this was his last show just before he came on air. To say the man didn't have his mind on the job is a fair statement. The last thing he was interested in was a book about the Australian

Outback, in fact I don't think he could have cared less about anything! So rather than us both sitting there silently, I told stories about the Outback and it became a storytime segment.

A few months after I arrived home I received a substantial cheque for appearing on the show which was a first. I had never been paid by any other telelvision station for an interview. Perhaps it was payment for keeping the show going with my storytelling!

I was staying in a beautiful old castle that had been converted to a hotel on the outskirts of Dublin. Unlike my cocoon back in London, my room here must have been the royal suite a few hundred years ago.

The day after the interview I was sitting in the foyer, waiting for the car to the airport, dreaming about living in such a castle. The concierge asked me if I would mind sharing my limousine to the airport with another guest whose car had not arrived. I said I didn't mind at all.

I sat on the back seat of the enormous car and a very old, distinguished gentleman was helped into the other side of the car. His assistant sat facing us. I smiled welcomingly and the older man let forth a barrage of French in the direction of his assistant.

I was weary, and a little upset about the way my tour had been handled. I had only ever experienced the complete professionalism of my Australian and New Zealand tours, and, quite frankly, I had expected the same from the English tour. And the fiasco of the sacked host on the last night of the tour—which was no-one's fault—really dampened my spirits. Now I was sharing my limo with a man who couldn't even give me a thank-you smile.

I turned away from them and stared out the window. I would be glad when I left for Austria, maybe they smile there, I thought.

More rapid French was exchanged and from the few words I could understand, I knew they were talking about me. I turned further away in defiance.

'Excuse me madam,' came to me in a beautiful accent. I turned towards the assistant with an expression of disinterest. He continued, 'Thank you for allowing us to ride in your car.'

'That's all right. There is plenty of room and it was my pleasure to be of assistance,' I replied and turned back to the window.

There was more French spoken then an older voice, in a similarly charming accent asked, 'You are not American?'

'No, I am Australian.' He then asked what I was doing in Ireland and what part of Australia I came from—was it Sydney? When I told him I lived in the Outback, the entire trip to the airport was filled with questions and the time passed quickly. I couldn't place this charming man's face but I was sure I had seen him somewhere.

When we arrived at the airport he said goodbye and was escorted away. While standing in line waiting to check-in for my flight, his assistant reappeared and said his boss wanted to express to me what an enjoyable conversation he had had with me and that he wished me well with my book.

'And what is your boss's name?'

He looked at me in amazement.

'I know his face,' I added, 'but just can't place him.'

'Why, my boss is Stephane Grappelli,' he said with a proud voice.

I felt such a fool. 'Please tell your boss I have enjoyed his music all my life!'

He smiled and departed.

What a ning-nong I was, not recognising a great man like that and not being able to tell him myself the enjoyment his music brings.

I landed back in London ready to leave the next day for Munich. That night I had a phone call from Marlee to say they were having blizzard conditions. Franz and Marlee had a four-hour drive to Munich to pick me up and if the weather didn't improve they wouldn't be able to get through the mountains near the Austrian border. It looked like I might have to stay in a hotel in Munich for the night. Another hotel! I could see my Austrian holiday being spent in a hotel in Munich waiting for the weather to lift.

Luckily the weather did improve and Marlee, Franz and Papa Ranacher met me and we headed for the border and Austria.

It was my first time in Germany and as we drove along the highway all I could see was cement and signs. I knew that somewhere behind the piled-up dirty snow, cement and signs were picture-book German villages. Hopefully I'll have time to see these beautiful villages one day, instead of just rushing by on an *Autobahn* (Freeway).

One sign kept flashing by at every exit, 'Ausgang'. After about the tenth sign, I finally asked Franz how big the town called Ausgang was as I had seen so many signs for it. He laughed heartily and told me that it was not the name of a town, but the German word for exit! He told Papa who also thought it was a great joke.

We came out of a long mountain tunnel into Austria and into the first sunshine I'd experienced since I left Australia! The sunlight sparkled on the white snow in the valley. Ice melted off bare tree branches and the branches of evergreens bowed with the weight of the fresh snow.

After driving through this fairyland of snow for hours, we arrived in Obermillstatt, a quaint little village nestled three thousand feet up on the side of a mountain and overlooking a frozen lake.

This is where I finished writing *Some of My Friends Have Tails*. My room had a big bay window which overlooked the lake and I would often wake from a reverie to realise I had just been sitting in front of my word processor doing nothing but soaking up the magical scene before me. After a few days I did settle down to the work at hand. As I'm used to getting up early, I worked from 4 a.m. to midday every day, and had the afternoons and weekends off.

A few days after I arrived, I received a frantic call from James in Sydney asking me not to go skiing. He was worried I might fall and break my leg as I had two tours that year, not to mention finishing a book. I laughed and said I was too busy writing. To put his mind at rest I told him I would play indoor tennis instead. As I only had a few ski lessons back in my youth, I already decided I would get the exercise I needed doing something I could do and loved.

I had a wonderful time playing tennis again, but like all things I do in my life, I went the whole hog and played first with Franz, then with Marlee, playing for an hour and a half almost nonstop. It was obvious to me after a few games that Franz was a natural. And I was sure Marlee would soon be up there with him through sheer determination. Once, that is, I had taught her to hit the ball in the court and not over the fence!

We had a great afternoon's tennis and I felt on top of the world after such a good workout. It was my first tennis in five years, and I hadn't realised how much I'd missed it.

The next morning told a different story. Every muscle was stiff and very sore. It took me ten minutes to get my clothes on and another five minutes to get up two flights of stairs to make it to breakfast. But being a sucker for punishment, I played tennis again that afternoon, as it was the only way to beat the stiffness. It was another four days before the stiffness was gone. Then the muscles came back to life and the soreness faded. I hadn't felt that good for years, and found it amusing to think I'd travelled halfway around the world to get some regular exercise.

Mama and Papa Ranacher had had a few English lessons before their visit to Bullo, but the rest of the family had virtually no English at all. Most of the people in the village

119

were in the same position, so we had more of the funny times we'd had when Mama and Papa visited Bullo.

Rosie, Franz's sister, offered to cut and dye my hair. She was a hairdresser so I knew I was in good hands. She called in during the week to ask me what colour dye I wanted for my hair. I had to explain I wanted a mixture of two dyes—chestnut and light brown. There was much laughter as we attempted to sort out the problem. We finally got the light brown part straight, but the chestnut was completely evading us. Finally Mama got out the German-English dictionary and I pointed to the German translation.

'Oh *Kastanie*, why didn't you say so!' was a rough translation of their reply . . . I think. The most important thing was that I got a wonderful haircut and the colour was just right.

I found everything about this part of Austria fascinating. We visited villages with nine-hundred-year-old churches and beautiful mountain streams which ran through stone watercourses and meandered through village squares. There were neat houses with flower boxes, empty now in winter, but I could imagine them full of brightly coloured flowers. Woodpiles were a work of art. I am sure some houses had another hidden pile of wood for burning, because the woodpiles didn't look like one piece of wood had been touched. We also visited Salzburg and Spittal which were nearby towns.

After I had trouble getting up the stairs after my first game of tennis, I was introduced to the world of the village sauna. Papa suggested a sauna and a massage would speed up my recovery.

People in Obermillstatt go to the sauna like people in Australia go to the TAB or the local club. Marlee had told me about the village sauna when she came back from Austria the previous year.

After Marlee and I undressed in the change room, we wrapped ourselves in towels and entered the sauna. Inside the door I came to a sudden halt with shock! Everyone was stark naked, men and women of all ages, shapes and sizes. They were all casually walking around, sitting reading magazines, or sitting at a bar on stools and drinking anything from health drinks to stout. Other people were sitting at tables, deep in conversation while sipping cofee. Marlee was enjoying herself immensely watching my reaction and eventually told me to stop gaping and led me into one of the steam rooms.

Marlee thought I would be more comfortable in a steam room as it was hard to see the other people. But the steam did clear every now and then before the next blast came in through the pipes, and I could see naked people sitting on benches having very normal conversations. Not one, as far as I could see, was the least bit worried by the fact that he or she was stark naked.

Having been raised in an Australian society which was uptight about sex, I was completely overwhelmed. I clutched my towel yet no-one even looked at me, other than a few glances that took in the towel and my expression that said 'tourist'.

121

After a few visits I calmed down and started to enjoy the sauna, but never relaxed to the point of shedding my towel.

My worst moment in the sauna came on my second visit—I was still nervous—when Marlee left me to go to the toilet. I quietly pleaded with her not to leave me alone. She told me to sit down, read a magazine and relax and she would be back in a minute. I decided she was right and was looking for somewhere to sit when a naked man walked straight up to me and started speaking to me in German. Talk about total panic. All my old-fashioned upbringing came rushing at me like a tidal wave. I couldn't believe I was standing in a sauna face-to-face with a naked man! My eyes darted everywhere in a vain effort not to look at him. My habit of looking down when I was thinking threw me into greater panic and had me throwing my head back in the air, looking at the ceiling and making strange sounds!

My brain sifted through the few German words I knew, but could only come up with, 'please', 'thank you', 'yes' and 'no'. I knew that except for 'no' these were all very dangerous words to reply to a question a naked man had asked me!

I finally stuttered out one word, 'English.'

Whereupon he said, 'Oh good, so am I.'

This upset me more, as somehow I thought it was alright to talk to a naked Austrian but not to a naked Englishman! And so up went the etiquette register!

It turned out he was looking for the exit, so I gladly told him, happy to have this knowledge.

Marlee walked up and jokingly chided me for talking to a naked man. I told her he just wanted the exit.

Upon hearing this she said, 'Mum! He had to get in

here, so he knows the same door gets him out. Besides, he was naked! I don't know, I leave you for a few minutes and you get picked up by a naked man!'

I didn't live that one down for a long time and Marlee told everyone the story with glee.

One of the most appealing things I came across in Austria were the cattle. In the winter all the animals are kept in barns or long sheds. I visited the Ranachers' five cows in their ninety-year-old barn. They were standing in a row contentedly chewing on their feed in a wooden box. Each of the cows' tails was held up by a piece of string which was connected to a spring, so when the cow sat down its tail could comfortably come down with it. The tail was elevated so it wouldn't get dirty if the cow sat down after it had deposited a pile of dung on the ground or fling it everywhere when it swished its tail. Dung was cleared away daily, but the cows often sat down and rested so it was expected that they regularly sat in dung or urine.

To stop the cows getting any skin problems during the winter months indoors, the animals were brushed every night. So you can imagine some of the amazed expressions on people's faces when they asked, 'And how many cattle do you have?'

When I replied 'Ten thousand', they would look at me with a dazed expression for a few seconds as they tried to visualise the sheds required to house this many cattle. Not to mention the staff, time and brushes required to brush them every night!

Mama and Papa live in a newly built house and Franz's brother Peter, his wife Guneula and their children Michael and Manuel now live in the four-hundred-year-old family home. Papa still uses the workshop in the old house for his hobby of making beautiful hand-made shoes. Entering the workshop is a journey back in time. It looks just like I imagine Santa's workshop does.

As much as I would have loved to explore everything about this fascinating country, the writing of the book took top priority. I had very little time when I got home to Bullo to put the second half together with the first half, which was being typed in Darwin by a typing agency. But I told myself, next time Vienna and the rest of Austria then on to Italy, France, Switzerland, Norway . . . the works!

Franz, Marlee and I left Obermillstatt together for Munich. They were flying home and I was flying to Frankfurt to meet my Qantas flight to Johannesburg to start my South African tour.

When I stepped on board the Qantas jumbo at Frankfurt I felt immediately at ease. Surrounded by the wonderfully familiar Australian accent, I felt at home for the first time since January.

CHAPTER 8

April
1995

I was looking forward to my first visit to South Africa, or any part of Africa, for that matter, as it has always held great fascination for me. I thought this would be a pleasant time, with only five days of touring in Johannesburg, Durban and Cape Town and a day off in Cape Town before I flew back to Johannesburg then home to Australia. What could go wrong? What indeed!

I arrived at nine o'clock at night looking forward to a nice early night and a good sleep in a bed.

But no. I was met at the airport by a hired publicity agent who belonged back in the days of the British Empire. She had the indomitable spirit that brought Britain through World War II. Bed at 9 p.m. at night? Good heavens, what was I thinking! No I had a three-hour radio show. I checked the three hours bit with her several times, but I had heard correctly. And there was no time beforehand to go to the hotel to have a quick shower and change.

I didn't dare ask what was happening after the radio show for fear there might be something! Besides I didn't get a chance. There was a running commentary happening on everything I needed to know about the rest of my tour.

We arrived at the radio building and heading for security parking under the building. As we approached the steel-barricaded entrance a nervous-looking guard was ordered to raise the screen. The car started to move into the building, but stalled. The screen reached the top and started to descend on the car. In the confusion that followed I gleaned the car was not the publicist's. There was high-level panic and chaos for the next twenty seconds as she issued orders to the guard at high 'C'. It turned out this was the guard's first night on duty and he didn't know how to stop the screen. The car wouldn't start, so the only thing I could think of was to jump out and push it. The guard and I were having great difficulty doing this, and I was screaming over the top high 'C' orders, 'Take off the bloody brake!'

The screen missed the car by a few feet and we watched as it hit the floor with a thud and locked into place behind us.

The next problem became clear when in imperialistic tones the guard was ordered to open the door into the building. This could be done with a key, but we didn't have one. He could open the door from the guard house, but that was now not possible as he was locked in the parking area and couldn't get out. It seemed the only way we could get out of the parking lot was to wait for someone else to enter or leave the building.

It was approaching my 9 p.m. radio session and we

had to agree there would be little traffic coming into the carpark at this time. We had to start thinking of alternatives. I thought the screen must have a handle to wind the door manually if there was a power failure. Our guard was very excited when he found the spot to do this, but we looked high and low and couldn't find the handle.

The guard came up with the next idea. He had a card which opened the door automatically, the only problem being you had to insert the card on the other side of the screen. He said he could ask a passer-by to insert it.

He did this. There was an endless exchange in their language, then the man walked away. We keenly cross-examined the guard who said the man said 'No'.

'No! All that talking and you say all he said was "no"!'

Apparently most of the time had been spent trying to find a dialect they could both understand. When they did, he couldn't convince the man we had locked ourselves in there accidentally. The other man's wise analysis of the situation was that we wouldn't be there if we weren't meant to be!

A few more appeals to passers-by had them just waving dismissively. I was wondering just where I had landed myself.

I finally sat back in the car thinking we probably wouldn't get out until someone in the building came down to their car to go home at midnight after the show.

I couldn't bear the thought of a three-hour conversation with the protector of the British Empire, so I opted for a sleep. I was dozing off to sleep, having successfully blocked out the constant stream of complaints, when headlights flashed into the carpark. The driver inserted a card into the machine and the screen magically started opening. Our saviour was the newsreader for our program.

The guard ducked under the rising screen and was extremely happy to be back at his post and out of complaints range. We followed the newsreader into the building and arrived at our destination five minutes late. You would imagine this wouldn't matter on a three-hour talk-back show, but you would think I was being presented to the Queen, the amount of fuss made.

The tour of England was about to get an A-1 rating compared to this one! I was wishing for my guardian angel, my Australian publicist Jane.

The talkback show had heavy religious overtones, with one of the first calls from a girl who said she didn't want to go on living and what did I suggest she do about it. The question really floored me. As you can imagine, I was feeling very tired at this point and in need of a hot shower, good food, clean clothes and some sleep. And here I was being asked to be an on-air psychologist! Being accustomed to having Jane with me, I looked for help from the publicist. But I could see her talking to a man a couple of studios away.

The radio host waited. I was in this by myself, it appeared. I started by saying I certainly wasn't qualified to discuss anything that serious, and I was sure there were organisations in Johannesburg that could help her. I went on to explain I had just landed in South Africa an hour ago, but would hand over to the host and she could give her some names of organisations that could help.

We both chatted with this poor girl, and I think she sounded a little better when we finished. But what a sad situation. For life to get you so down, you have no desire to continue living. I expressed this thought and it led to some very interesting discussions over the next hour or so.

It was a thoroughly exhausting evening and I felt completely drained. When the publicist asked if I would like to go for a drink, she got a loud, 'No!'

I finally made it to my room. There were no complicated instructions here, just a good old-fashioned key. But I seemed to have a surplus. I sat and examined the pile of keys I had been given. Everything in the room that opened had a key to lock it. I was instructed to lock everything or it would be stolen.

I had faced this same situation when I first went to Manila in 1960. I watched in amazement when the next-door neighbour locked all the servants out of the house every time she went out! They sat in the servants' quarters until she returned.

I decided to do the opposite and left everyone in the house and told my house girls to take care of everything while I was gone. In all the years I lived there, I always returned to the house exactly as I left it.

I must admit this time I succumbed to the instructions the first time I left the room. But after locking, forgetting something, unlocking, then locking up again only to find I needed something else, just trying to leave my room on time became a major trauma. So when faced with the task the next day, I stayed in bed an extra fifteen minutes and thought, stuff the keys.

As I was rushing down the hall that morning I saw the housemaid cleaning one of the other rooms. I stopped and told her I was running late, and could she please take care of my room for me as I didn't have time to lock any cupboards. She gave me a smile that would make your heart sing, and said, 'Yes, ma'am.'

I had a ten-hour day which finished with a delightful dinner with Pan Macmillan people and business friends, turning it into a fifteen-hour day.

The next day was a typical book-promotion day, with an early-morning television talkshow, interviews with newspaper reporters, a literary luncheon and an evening talk to a professional women's club.

The evening was supposed to be a big night. The bookseller had arranged hundreds of books in an impressive display and he even had a cash register. There were rows and rows of chairs—enough to seat hundreds— and a long table filled with all types of cocktail food.

Only six people turned up to the badly organised event! And the bookseller silently packed up his display and left without a word.

When the publisher called the next day and asked how the night went, I told him the sales were 150 per cent and he was over the moon, 'How many people were there?' was his next excited question. When he heard the answer he was furious.

I prayed the rest of the tour wouldn't follow the same

path. I was used to Australian organisation, but I was a long way from home so I had to make the best of it. After all, the luncheon had been successful, I told myself.

The next morning I left my room in the faithful hands of the housemaid and it was off to morning tea and a book signing. When I got back to the hotel to pack for Durban, I gave my room guardian a large tip. I left the hotel with everything I arrived with and I never locked anything but the door to my room. The essence of trust in another human being came through loud and clear.

I was in South Africa at an interesting time with apartheid now a thing of the past. In Durban I stayed in a lovely old house in a previously restricted section of the beautiful city. The streets were crowded with people walking—simply because they could.

Cape Town was breathtaking as we approached it from the air. But on the drive from the airport to the city, behind concrete walls, slums stretched into the distance. Cape Town by comparison is amazingly opulent, full of stately homes and gardens. I was staying in a guest house in the shadow of Table Mountain.

By Cape Town the tour had settled into its own groove. Not what I had expected, but luckily it was developing its own momentum. There was one more day to go.

I spoke at the University of Cape Town in the morning and had lunch at the famous pink Nelson Hotel. We were driven there by a delightful reporter who informed us she didn't have a licence, so I spent the entire ride fully occupied with pointing out cars to avoid.

By the time we reached the gates of the hotel, it wasn't too much of a mystery why she didn't have a licence. I breathed a sigh of relief thinking, 'Safe, for the time being.'

As we approached the hotel a good portion of the grounds and the main entrance had a cordon of soldiers with lethal-looking guns.

Our eccentric reporter, busy talking, drove between the soldiers and pulled up at the hotel's front entrance. Suddenly twenty guns were pointing at the small car, and us!

Guns have been a part of my life since I came to live in the Outback, but I can tell you this day my heart stopped beating and hit the floor with a thud. But my companions were made of stauncher stuff with a lifetime of guns being pointed in their faces. The reporter simply asked, 'What is going on?'

She was told there was a press conference luncheon for Nelson Mandela and all the area was restricted. I thought that was an ironic remark, and I am sure the officer had the slightest hint of a smile on his face, but this went over the others' heads.

As we parked at the far end of the large courtyard, a big shiny limo pulled up at the entrance, right in the spot where we had sat a minute earlier with twenty or so guns trained on us. And James said it was too dangerous for me to ski in Austria!

My last day in Cape Town was perfect; we visited a wine-growing district and had lunch in a delightful restaurant overlooking a valley of vineyards. There was perfect sunshine, and the food was out of this world and our host for the day could not have been more accommodating in any way. If I believed in past lives, I would have to say my heart belongs to Africa in another lifetime, so strong was the physical pull this land exerted on me. I flew to Johannesburg that evening, was back at the hotel with my room guardian, and the next day stepped on board a Qantas flight for home!

After a meeting in Sydney I flew back to Bullo. After two months away it was so good to be home and the dogs gave me the usual royal welcome. Boots, unfortunately, was not well and I was shocked when I saw how terribly thin he was. Marlee said he looked good compared to two weeks before when she arrived home. When Marlee first saw him he was in such bad condition she thought it was too late to save him. But he came up to her and was so glad to see her, she knew she had to try and save him.

Franz flew Sarah, our vet, out to the station and she gave him a series of injections and filed what teeth he had left so he could get some chewing power from a more even bite.

It only took a few days of being handfed all day and continued vitamin and antibiotics injections before he started to pick up. We kept handfeeding for the next few months—and didn't he lap that up!

133

It took around six months to get him back to the reasonably fat, healthy horse we had left in January but the most important thing was he was back to his old self.

Sarah said a good part of the problem could have been he missed his family. The caretaker gave him food and water, but he didn't treat Boots as a person like we did, so that would upset him. I put a note in my diary to get a horse lover as our next caretaker.

Halfway through March we began getting thrilling results from the breast cancer prevention campaign. Letters started arriving from women who were going for a mammogram for the first time! I hoped this trend was here to stay.

As is often the case, this good news was followed by bad. Sarah, our vet, who had struggled so hard to start her clinic in Kununurra was about to go into hospital for an operation and she couldn't find a vet to take over her practice for the month she needed to take off to recover.

When Marlee heard of the problem she decided to look for a good Samaritan vet. It took a few days, but she finally found a wonderful vet from Darwin who left his practice in good hands and went down to Kununurra and kept Sarah's new practice going.

Here was one human being helping another. A complete stranger in this case, who refused to accept any payment for his time. Such a story restores my faith in humanity and shows how wonderful people can be.

In my eyes Sarah deserved this kindness because she cares so deeply for all the animals in her care. She saved our beautiful Sumie! She justly deserved a guardian angel to help her through a difficult period in her life. And my guardian angel found him for her.

A letter arrived from Pan Macmillan South Africa at this time giving me news on how the book was faring. It was accompanied by media clippings and reviews. The results were good—the book made number one on the bestseller list, and the sales were still going strong, even approaching the sales of a Wilbur Smith book, which really amazed me. It goes to show that if the readers like a book, it will sell regardless of whether a tour is well-organised or not.

Near the end of March I headed for the east coast for a short tour for the paperback of *The Strength In Us All*. This was combined with a speaking tour of capital cities with a group of Australian and American speakers.

I was looking forward to watching American speakers at close quarters. As much as I don't want to make the speaker's circuit my entire life, the aim of most speakers is to get onto the American speaking circuit. I wanted to study the speakers and see what talents attracted amounts like twelve-thousand American dollars. This amount was for a run-of-the-mill speaker. Astronauts and retired Presidents got six-figure fees!

I was in the company of some great Australian speakers, Amanda Gore and Allan Pearse. I have spoken at conferences with them around Australia and never tire of listening to them. I just tell a story but these two are top performers. Hazel Hawke and Peter McKeon were also in the Australian group.

I was not impressed with the American speakers and the Australian speakers seemed to be the most popular with the audiences. We spoke in Sydney, Melbourne and Brisbane and while the rest of the speakers had the day off in between travelling from one capital to the next, I rushed off and did book promotions in the towns close to each capital city.

I had fallen back into the bad habit of trying to do everything requested of me and tension was taking over again. Of course I didn't admit this to myself. Although it should have been blatantly clear to me when a dear friend of mine in Melbourne came backstage to say hello and I didn't know her name! My thought process was such that I thought anyone backstage had to be connected with the tour. So Fairlie received some strange answers to her questions until I realised my error. In my defence, backstage was an experience and there were people going in all directions, so when Fairlie's face appeared, I recognised it immediately, just couldn't find a name to go with it for a few seconds.

Appointments, travelling around the eastern states and short breaks in Caloundra took up the rest of the month and I arrived home the 28th April. I met Marlee in Darwin as she was in town to have the dreaded six-monthly check-up again. We went home to Bullo together to wait and worry until the results came through. Once again, they were all-clear, much to our relief.

CHAPTER 9

May 1995 –
September 1995

May was full of film offers for book number one. I have often read stories about writers not having any business sense. This belief must be widespread, as some of the contracts I received were laughable. One contract offered me five hundred dollars in return for a world option on my story. The man called a few days later wanting to know why I hadn't contacted him to take up his offer!

I have been receiving offers since the first week the book was released and have quite a file now. But I am a bit stubborn. So until I read a fair contract—for me—they will keep piling up in the file. Meanwhile, I am learning a lot about film contracts and what not to sign.

Before long I was off to Sydney to do a Qantas advertisement, to Melbourne to speak for a charity, back to Sydney for another fundraiser then onto Fiji for a business conference. I came home from Fiji through Sydney and it took another four days before I managed to make it to Bullo.

When I returned I was home for two months! I locked myself in the office for many reasons—the mustering season was beginning, the accountant needed figures and piles of mail had to be opened. From August onwards it would be back to non-stop appointments until December, as it had been each year. I sat down and tried to work out why each year the last six months just seem to spin out of control.

While I liked to think the reason I was at home for so long was to get my life under control, the real reason could have been that we were having so many people to visit. Our first visitors were family. Ever since I moved to Bullo I have tried to get my sister Susan to visit. I had never succeeded—she wouldn't come anywhere near the place. I can understand this attitude in the early years, but lately Bullo has become a nice place to visit. So her husband Ralph and I thought if he and my brother Tod came, Susan might join them. The big surprise was that Frances, Tod's wife, wanted to come. Fran is such a gentle soul I just thought the wilds of Bullo would not interest her in the least, so I was delighted when she said she would love to visit.

I ended up with Ralph, Tod, Frances, and an old family friend, Don McFadden, but no Susan. They all had a great time and I enjoyed their visit so much. Ralph went home saying our plan to get Susan to Bullo had failed, but he had a great holiday trying to achieve it!

They left the day before we had twenty-two New Zealand cattlemen and women for the day including a sit-down lunch. There was only time for a deep breath in between the family's departure, drafting cattle in the yards and the arrival of our new guests. We mustered cattle during the family visit and were still drafting when the New Zealanders were here. We trucked our first load of sale cattle for the season the day after their departure.

Mustering and sales of cattle usually start as soon as the weather permits us to open our road—around April or May. This year we were waiting for cattle prices to improve, but it was evident they were not going to, so we started moving cattle.

No sooner had the dust, churned up by the wheels of the road train settled, than Marlee and Franz were planning to go to Queensland in the plane to the Dundee Cattle Stud. A good year or so before, I had received a phone call from Frank Fraser. Mr Fraser is one of Queensland's great cattlemen, but age was catching up with him and he had decided with regret he would have to sell his beloved stud. He had read my book and decided that the Dundee cattle should move to Bullo River and stay intact. I knew of the Dundee Stud and its exceptional line of cattle, in fact Mr Fraser's previous stud was Burnside and some of the first breeding bulls Marlee and I purchased were Burnside bulls.

Mr Fraser might have been slowing down physically, but his business brain wasn't suffering the same fate! He was a great wheeler-dealer and could sense my weakness. He knew there was a deal there if he just kept at it, and he did!

I knew I couldn't afford the whole Dundee herd, as much as I would have liked to transfer it intact to Bullo. I casually asked what he was looking at for the whole herd and dropped the phone in fright, even though I thought I was thinking big. This was more than big money and I was relieved to hear that it included the land. He was another person who thought because you have a book published you are immediately worth millions. I told him it was out of my league and thanked him for calling.

But Mr Fraser had it in his head that his herd was going to Bullo and he quickly realised he had a keen ally in Marlee. After that he called regularly and between Mr Fraser, Marlee and Franz, I was worn down. Of course I wanted these beautiful cattle as much as Marlee and Franz did, but it seemed I was the only one thinking about how to get the money to pay for them. The enthusiasm of youth won through and so we took up the opportunity to get some marvellous blood lines into our herd.

So it was decided as soon as the opportunity presented itself, Marlee and Franz would fly to Queensland to buy a few of the Dundee line—not the whole herd, just a few. I kept repeating this to them parrot-fashion at every opportunity before their departure. Knowing full well that Marlee would get there, fall in love with every animal in sight and I would receive rapturous calls about the beautiful cattle, and couldn't we just ... But there was a lot of work to be done before they left.

After the movement of our first load of cattle, the mustering season had officially begun. There is a huge cost involved in employing staff, overhauling machines, checking and repairing fences, and in some situations, building roads. So once the mustering starts, we go flat out, every day, until the mustering is done. Other work on the station has to wait or is done at the beginning or end of the season.

This season started as they always do, with new people trying to fit into the way of life of the Outback, and trying to make themselves into a team.

Each year we work very hard to keep people safe from any dangerous encounters. But these inevitably seem to happen. This year it was not one of the budding stockmen who ended up nose to nose with a raging wild beast, but a sixteen-year-old girl!

Eleisha had arrived at Bullo in June, but not via the normal hiring channels. At a conference in Sydney I had been totally engrossed in signing the books being thrust at me from every angle, when the sea of women seemed to part to reveal a lone man. His eyes held sadness and a hint of desperation. I put the desperation down to the fact he was feeling uncomfortable and out of place. I meet a lot of men in this position. They are usually there because their wife for some reason can't attend and so she sends hubby along to get her book signed. I assumed this man was on this type of mission.

But it turned out he was asking for help. He had a young daughter who loved the land and the family had recently sold their farm and moved closer to the city. She was not adapting well, and was becoming almost

141

impossible to handle. A bright intelligent girl, her school grades were slipping, she was drifting into bad company and her family was at a loss to know what to do next.

I felt the desperation of this man, but I expressed my concern about our ability to handle such a problem. We had our hands full just running the property and training older, willing staff and keeping them out of danger. A rebellious teenager wasn't something I'd take on lightly! But when he ended up on his knees, I knew I had to help if it was possible.

We had long discussions over the phone and Marlee talked to Eleisha and explained what life was like on Bullo. In very clear words we said if she stepped out of line, just once, or didn't do as we asked, she would be on the next plane home.

Having firmly established the rules, we asked Eleisha to write us a letter saying why she wanted to come to Bullo and what she thought she would gain from the experience. After receiving her letter we took the plunge and said yes, she could come for the season.

The cattle were in the yards and were being drafted, so Marlee put Eleisha where she thought she would be safe—on top of a five-foot-tall bale of hay. The bale was round and slippery and it required a certain amount of dexterity to stay on it. All the animals had been drafted out of the yard except a strong mickey bull who didn't want to go anywhere. He had his head in between the bale and the corner of the yard and was working on the theory that if he couldn't see them, they couldn't see him! Cattle are mustered into the yards for many reasons; for branding, cutting of mickey weaners (young bulls castrated to become steers), culling of the herd, and drafting of sale cattle. So this mickey bull didn't know what was ahead of him—castrating—but was behaving as if he knew.

He was also taking his anger out on the steel rails, headbutting them repeatedly, in between pawing the ground and snorting loudly. When only one animal is left in a pen it becomes very hard to handle. They want nothing to do with you, are frightened and the last thing they have on their minds is cooperation!

Eleisha was poking him with a length of poly pipe, hoping to make him decide to turn around and go out of the corner. He swung his head at her in annoyance and she was surprised by the swiftness and the strength of the movement. The piece of poly went flying through the air, Eleisha reeled backwards in fright, her feet went out from under her and she slipped down the side of the hay bale, hitting the ground with a thud.

She now found herself in the corner of the yards, right in front of the young bull. Closed in by steel rails and a quarter of a tonne of hay, her only exit was blocked by the very mad mickey she had just been poking! Everyone in the yards stopped what they were doing and rushed to her aid. If they hadn't seen her fall, her screams certainly alerted them to the problem. Marlee shouted instructions to the team as she rushed to Eleisha's aid.

Being face to face with a wild bull, big or small, is a paralysing experience, no matter how long you have worked with wild cattle. So you can imagine how a sixteen-year-old girl who'd never been exposed to

143

anything wilder than a tame milking cow would feel. The general consensus of the people within earshot was that Eleisha's screams were so piercing, they scrambled the mickey's brain.

The young bull was turning in confused circles intent on getting away from the noise. Wild-eyed, he shook his head, stamped his feet, and tried everything to dislodge the noise in his ears. The first thing he saw was Eleisha's backside as she jumped, screaming, to her feet. He had found the source of the deafening noise! So he lowered his head and tried to fling her out of earshot. He was only a small bull and the result was that Eleisha ended up sitting on the mickey's head, going up and down like a seesaw.

The screaming continued, so the mickey increased his efforts to rid himself of the offending noise and Eleisha's seesaw ride increased. Orders were shouted for her to grab the top rail of the fence on her way up so she could then swing out of the yard. But the terror of actually sitting on the head of a wild bull meant she was really beyond listening to any advice let alone carrying it out. Besides, it was impossible for her to hear any instructions over her screaming. As soon as the mickey saw a way out, he took off at high speed with his ears wildly flapping, desperately attempting to stop the terrible noise.

It took a while to calm Eleisha, and when she realised it was over, she started laughing, crying and screaming all at once. And I am sure if the mickey heard this amazing combination of sound he would have increased his speed to make sure of his escape.

As serious and dangerous as the incident was, everyone couldn't help laughing at the expression on the mickey's face and his efforts to get away from the frightening noise and Eleisha. Everyone agreed Eleisha had saved herself, just by screaming. They were all quite confident if no-one had been there to help her the mickey would have still run away to save his ears.

It took quite a while for Eleisha to regain her composure, which was very understandable. All the colour had drained from her face, her complexion remained very pale for many hours to come. After a thorough examination Marlee declared Eleisha clear of any serious injury. There were some minor cuts and quite a few bruises surfaced in the next few days, but apart from these, strained vocal cords were her most serious problem. Luckily, the bull's horns had just been tipped, which would also account for his bad temper and the frustration displayed when he repeatedly failed to hook Eleisha with the missing tips of his horns.

I feel the mickey bull experience along with helping save the life of a newborn foal were turning points in Eleisha's young life. Most people never have one of these experiences, and Eleisha had both of them in a matter of a few months. Interspersed along the way with Marlee's wise counsel whenever she went off track or had doubts about where she was heading.

Facing death has a very sobering effect on anyone and I know she must have been thinking, 'What if I had died in there, what would I have regretted in this short life of mine?'

Eleisha was hardly over the meeting of the ways with her young bull when Marlee brought one of our favourite mares, Gold, home into the garden. She had just given birth that morning and Marlee felt she was a bit down in condition and decided she needed a few weeks of TLC. The foal seemed all right, just a little weak.

Everyone went to work in the yards and when Marlee returned at lunchtime the foal was lying on the ground fighting for its life. The change in a few hours had been dramatic. Eleisha offered to help Marlee with the tiny creature and Marlee showed her how to dribble a special mixture, which contained substances to quickly hydrate the foal, into its mouth.

Marlee and Sarah, our vet, who was now back at work, came to the opinion the foal had an infection in the umbilical cord. It was also completely dehydrated from collapsing on the ground in the sun. So the foal was carefully moved to a cool place and the rest of the day was devoted to getting as much liquid down its throat as possible. Marlee gave it a penicillin injection to bring the cord infection under control.

All afternoon the foal hovered close to death and Marlee could see another night without sleep, trying to save this life of only a few days.

Over the many years on the station, a sleepless night to save the life of an animal has not been an unusual event. We have walked out the night with horses suffering colic, sat with animals with new stitches to stop them tearing open their wounds. Talked the night through with dairy cows with difficult births and comforted favourite fillies with first foals. Eleisha offered to

146

do the night shift and Marlee, feeling decidedly weary, after mustering and drafting for fourteen hours, accepted. Marlee told her if she needed any help, or was worried about something, to wake her immediately.

Eleisha rolled out her swag and took up her position next to the foal. All night she talked to the tiny creature, encouraging it to fight for its life. Having been in the same position many times I know she must have told the foal all her dreams, her fears and her secrets as she gazed at the endless heaven of stars. I know this magic of Outback nights well, as it has woven its spell over me so many times. Words fail to capture the floating feeling that courses through your body and mind when at the end of a long night those beautiful eyes open and look up into your eyes and say 'Thank you'.

The look on Eleisha's face the next morning as she proudly kneeled next to the very wobbly foal, and Marlee said she had saved that beautiful horse's life, was something to behold.

By the end of the season Eleisha had decided to become a vet. She went back home and returned to school at the beginning of the next year.

Snakes were bad this season. When cleaning the house and staff quarters—which are unoccupied for six months—we occasionally come across king brown snakes. This year the first one sighted was near the homestead. The two girls sharing the house duties and cooking were lugging yet another load of washing out to the clothesline. Gail, our New Zealander, spotted a snake in the still-uncompleted—fifteen years to date—squash court.

They called Marlee who rushed for the shotgun and told them to keep an eye on the snake.

Marlee came running back with the gun and was horrified to find one girl in serious battle with a seven-foot king brown. This snake had just come up a flight of steel steps at an alarming speed and Myra was trying to block its escape by poking it with a mop! This is not the best thing to do to a cornered killing machine—but Marlee had said to keep it in the squash court and that was what she intended doing.

Marlee watched astonished as the snake didn't bother to attack, but was only intent on avoiding the mop and escaping to the safety of the long grass under the clothesline. The grass had been mown recently and this was the only cover for a fair distance. Now the snake was on home ground it would be a different story if it was approached with a mop, so Marlee warned Myra not to pursue it.

There was a great discussion between the two girls about how they were going to get the snake out of the grass. The thought of carrying out a load of washing to the clothesline and having a king brown jump out of the grass at you was not a pleasant thought. Especially if you had just whacked it several times over the head with a mop!

The girls looked to Marlee for the answer. She told them to sit silently and watch. The minutes passed and the girls watched in amazement as eventually a large head slowly appeared above the long grass and looked around to see if the coast was clear. They then watched in even greater amazement as Marlee took aim and the snake's head exploded before their eyes. A convulsing, headless body thrashed its way out of the long grass and came to a halt on the short grass not far from their feet.

The girls let out a long-held breath and headed for the less-exciting chores of dishes and dusting. They were both sure they would never hang out washing again without remembering the washing day with a difference at Bullo.

We never kill snakes out in the bush: it is their territory and we respect that. But the homestead is our territory and we have to discourage poisonous snakes. So there are only a few acres which are off limits and they have the rest of the half a million acres to roam free.

I really believe that over the years the snakes have come to respect this rule. When we first arrived there were snakes everywhere and it was not unusual to shoot ten or more a season. If you look carefully around the homestead you can see evidence of shotgun-pellet damage on the walls, on the tree trunks that used to hold up the roof, on various doors and, in some cases, on the furniture. These days we can go the whole season without sighting a king brown. A couple of pythons usually wander through the house, but that's about it. And although your heart skips a beat when you switch on the light and see something slithering across the floor, as soon as you see the lovely iridescent flashes of colour your heart goes back to normal and you wait for it to be on its way.

So the season was on its way with the first sighting of a king brown. Marlee was confident she had the beginnings of a good team with these two girls and she was right. They had spunk. Not too many people would stand up to a king brown with a mop. We also had three very good stockmen which was fortunate because we needed good people if we were to get through the work we had so courageously planned during the wet season.

The first major setback of the season was our troublesome cubing machine. Franz, with the help of Bill Wilson, a mechanic from Darwin, was determined to unravel the problems of the machine. He had done a lot of reading over the wet season and was convinced the hydraulics were at fault. Much of the wiring was not according to the manual—there had been a lot of makeshift repairs done to the machine before we received it.

The mechanic we sent to New South Wales to look at the machine for us before we bought it said it had just come out of the field from working when he inspected it. What arrived at Bullo was definitely not a working machine. When Franz took it apart for cleaning and inspection he found barbwire inside the barrel, where the pellets are formed. So the mechanic had either spent his time in the pub, or the machine he inspected was not the machine we received. Either way we had been taken to the cleaners. We thought that paying for a mechanic to travel south to inspect the machine should have protected us. We were wrong. But we learnt another good lesson. If you want something done do it yourself and stay with the machine until it is on your property.

After four thousand dollars worth of parts it was looking hopeful that the machine might work. The repairs were completed on the hydraulic system, and we were ready for the first big test. Marlee was very excited when she presented me with the first cubes. So was I, just quietly. I thought it would always be a dream we never achieved, but there in my hand were compressed biscuits of feed. This amazing process happened while the machine was chugging along the rows of cut hay. It scooped up the hay at one end and spat out biscuits at the other.

At 8.30 that night one of the staff remarked how red the sky was behind the staff quarters. This immediately galvanised Franz and Marlee into action because that was the opposite direction to where the sun set—in the direction of the hay field and our now operating cuber!

Franz and all the crew drove into the field, which was burning fiercely and started to put out the fire on the cuber. Marlee had stopped at the workshop and jumped into the grader and headed for the fire. She graded a firebreak around the cuber, then another break around the burning field to try and contain the fire and save the rest of the hay. Everyone had a busy evening which finished late, but they managed to save the cuber and the rest of the hay field.

The morning revealed a semicircle of burnt hay with the cuber standing forlornly in the middle. All the work on the hydraulic system had literally gone up in smoke, only two days after it was all installed! There was about ten thousand dollars worth of damage.

Some machines are bad luck. Since the cuber's

151

purchase we had cleaned, checked and oiled the machine and replaced parts to bring it back to its original working state. This machine, in my opinion, was not meant to be ours. I just knew it belonged somewhere else and was wishing at that point in time it would just disappear, leaving behind all the money it had cost us in a neat little pile on the ground!

Unfortunately the cuber didn't go anywhere. It just sat in the workshop in a miserable, burnt state waiting for more work to be done. The plan of cubing the hay was now out of the question so it was back to baling it. We had already baled most of the hay and the plan had been to just do a few of the paddocks in cubes, so luckily there wasn't much to do.

No sooner had the fire been conquered than Boots had an accident. This horse had more accidents than any animal or human I have ever known. This time he cut his leg just behind the hoof and had come limping into the garden with blood pouring everywhere.

Marlee applied a pressure bandage and it stopped the bleeding. But after a few hours it started again and just kept bleeding. Marlee tried another pressure bandage but to no avail—he had cut a small vein and she knew by now the only way she was going to stop the blood flow was to find the vein and try and stitch it together.

It was 1 a.m. by this time and Gail had been sitting with Boots up to this point. Too valuable and skilled in all the outside work Marlee had quickly moved Gail from housework. Gail also loved anything to do with animals, especially horses. Boots had charmed her completely, so she willingly gave up a night's sleep to help.

This horse had been through so many dramas with us he knew when he was being helped and was always very cooperative. What Marlee achieved in the next hour was remarkable, and possible only because she was working on Bootsie boy. She injected a local anaesthetic around the cut as Gail held a torch. So he couldn't move around while she was working, Marlee had one of Bootsie's legs in a sling. So he was standing on three legs, including the injured leg. She finally found the bleeding vein and with extreme difficulty managed to get two stitches into the vein and stopped the bleeding.

Boots was so weak near the end of the operation from loss of blood he leaned most of his weight on Marlee or Gail and one stage nearly fell on top of Marlee while she was working.

Marlee gave him another injection for the pain, put on his rug to keep him warm and Gail stayed with him for the rest of the night to keep him company.

The next morning Gail was very weary but a happy, limping Boots greeted Marlee ready for his next meal. Marlee gave him another painkiller, in case he was in pain, but he appeared calm and gave no indication of being distressed in any way.

I think he enjoyed having Gail sit with him all night and lapped up every minute of the attention he received during his hospitalisation in the garden until the cut healed. Then he was let out to chase his favourite fillies and get into another mess!

153

Meanwhile the new season was maintaining a blistering pace with some of the men cutting hay, the jillaroos trucking it back to the storage yard, Franz and Marlee taking turns flying the plane to Darwin for various urgent spare parts and different people coming to the station for a wide variety of reasons. The truck was also taken to town regularly to pick up parts and equipment too heavy for the plane. When not flying, Marlee was grading the road or fence clearing on the bulldozer, or building fences with the rest of the crew.

I was putting the finishing touches on my third book and selecting the photos.

During my two months at home in June and July I watched our new people for the season jell into a good operational team. They worked together smoothly, quite capable of handling all the problems that were coming their way.

With the team fully occupied with a long fence line to complete Marlee and Franz headed for Queensland and the Dundee Stud to look at cattle to buy. Franz was also planning a quick trip to Sydney to look at a cement truck we had the opportunity to buy.

Marlee managed to control her urge to buy all the cattle at the stud and stuck to what we had agreed. Not that she didn't try to convince me that more would be better! The arrangements were made for the road trains to pick up our precious cargo and Marlee waved goodbye to our beautiful new cattle as they left on their across-Australia journey. The cattle would have a three-day rest in Cloncurry and be dipped and spend another day in Katherine, making it a long journey. The rests are not only kind to the cattle but extremely necessary or they will get footsore. And a breeding bull with sore feet is not the thing!

We were well into the drafting of the next muster when the road trains with the Dundee cattle arrived. Their two rests on the long journey across Australia had them looking well considering they had travelled thousands of miles. We had sorghum hay waiting for them in the yard and they were straight into it. These cattle had been in drought conditions for a long period of time and it had been a long while since they had seen hay the likes of Bullo home-grown sorghum. They stayed in the yards and ate for most of the day, only sitting down to rest after the sun had gone down.

Another giant leap forward in fulfilling Charlie's dreams happened when the Dundee cattle stepped onto Bullo country. These animals had the very best of Brahman blood running in their veins. Decades of devoted breeding was standing quietly in our yards munching on hay. We were very excited and couldn't wait to see our first calves.

The drafting of the cattle from the muster was finished and the sale cattle were loaded onto the same trucks that brought in the Dundee cattle, saving us some freight costs.

Right on schedule Marlee and most of the staff were off to the Katherine Show. Marlee was about to introduce

Bazza, our Bazadaise breeding bull we were so excited about, to the cattlemen and women of the North!

Bazza behaved himself at the show despite the fact he'd only had ten days out of the paddock to be spruced up and learn showring manners. He carried off his first parade with flying colours, only letting out a few dignified snorts and doing one joyful leap into the air with a massive kick, just to show how happy he was to be at the show.

I was sceptical about the chances of a French bull taking out a prize in the rugged Outback. I could already hear the jokes about a French bull on a cattle station run by women! But I was wrong. The cattle at the shows in the North are almost always Brahman, so there are only the two categories—the Brahmans and other breeds. And Bazza walked away with first prize in the other breeds division! Although I do have to add that all the judges were from interstate, so we still don't know what the North really thinks of our French bulls. However a lot of the men mosied over to Bazza's pen during the Show and gave him a thorough once-over while they thought no-one was looking.

The day Bazza won first prize Franz flew to Darwin to pick up Robert, a school friend of his and Papa Ranacher. Papa seemed to like Bullo. He was here on his second visit to help Franz with the welding of the new horse yards we were planning to build. These new yards would come complete with a roof over the round yard, so at last we would be able to work with horses in the wet season.

Franz and the stockmen had been cementing in the posts and cutting the lengths of steel for yard rails and gates. Papa Ranacher was a master welder before he retired and just between you and me I think he missed being involved with large steel projects.

But before it was down to work, there was a bit of sightseeing for our guests. We wanted to buy some young heifers and Newcastle Waters Station was having their yearly sale. We decided to fly over and see what was on offer. Papa was doing well: he had only been in the country two days and had already visited the Katherine Show, been to the annual Brahman dinner and was now off to Newcastle Waters, just south of Katherine.

There were some lovely lines of young heifers but the export trade of heifers to the Philippines was at its peak and there were buyers there trying to fill their export orders. We dropped out of the bidding at around three hundred dollars plus per head and it was still going furiously as we walked away. We had planned to stay the night which would have been necessary to arrange the trucking of cattle purchased. But with no purchases we decided to fly home. We rushed out to the airstrip and just made it home to Bullo before last light.

During this time my friend and speaking agent, Christine Maher, came to visit. Christine was flying to Perth and she decided since she was almost here, she would

take a break and head north. She was going on an organised safari from Broome to Kununurra where we would
pick her up and bring her out to the station for a few
days before she headed home to Sydney. An overland
safari in the Outback of northern Australia just didn't fit
with Christine. So after we had talked about these plans
for months, I finally voiced my concerns. I could sense
the excitement in her voice and I didn't want to dampen
this enthusiasm. But I was assured this was a very up-
market safari and so the subject was forgotten.

When Christine stepped out of the plane at Bullo she
looked stunned. Her up-market safari had included a
shovel for the toilet and bathing out in the open out of
a billy can. I think she arrived at Bullo terrified she
would find more of the same. A grateful smile spread
over her face when she saw a room with a bed in it and
her own bathroom with a flushing toilet! After a few
delicious meals cooked by Marlee she was back to
normal and very glad the safari was behind her.

Our next important arrival was our new sheds! A prime
mover towing two trailers fully loaded with forty tonnes
of new equipment sheds and an aircraft hangar arrived
on schedule with no hassles on the entire journey from
Dubbo to Bullo. So we were busy all day unloading
prefab sheds and entertaining guests in the evening.

During this time I was approached by a television station
to host a new weekly program. As much as I would

158

have loved to have been involved, it was physically and logistically impossible. Running a half a million acre cattle station usually keeps a person fully occupied for a whole year. Writing a book every fifteen months could also be viewed as a full-time occupation. Add to this conference speaking, book tours each year and regular directors' meetings and I was finding it difficult to visit my family or take a holiday.

The thought of fitting in forty-six weeks of filming was totally beyond me and I said so. They said they would work around my schedule! They obviously had no idea what my schedule looked like.

Considering I was already away from home on average eight months of the year, the arithmetic didn't work. It seemed I would need twenty-two months in my year to do the show. So I declined.

Handling thousands of head of cattle, problems are always present and this season was no exception. We had yarded three thousand cattle and were just over a day into the drafting. Eight hundred cows had been released back into the big holding paddock and the process of drafting the rest of the young heifers and cows out into this paddock was almost complete. Next, the very young calves would be branded so they could be released into the paddock and pair up with their mums for a feed.

Then the drafting of cows and calves would have been finished. But two bulls changed that idea. These two decided to have a knockdown, haul-out fight. The power of two thousand pound wild bulls in combat is something to be seen. Only the naked eye can appreciate the energy of solid muscle slamming into solid muscle.

These two bulls in question were taking all their frustration out on each other and there was nothing anyone could do except watch. One launched himself at his opponent and their massive heads connected. His opponent was slightly off-balance and his muscles gave way sending him backwards at tremendous speed. He quickly ran out of space in the pen and his backside came up against the steel panel of the portable yard with colossal force. They both hit the fence with a mighty whoosh, the force snapping off the lugs holding the steel pins that held the panels together.

The two panels sagged open but were still standing, but not for long. The attacking bull saw he had his opponent off-balance and in he went again. The next charge saw the two bulls explode into the steel fence sending panels flying through the air like frisbees. With two panels gone the rest of the section went down like dominoes.

In a few seconds a whole side of the main receiving yard was lying flat and eighteen hundred cattle were released into our just-released, drafted cows.

Luckily the mustering chopper had gone to a job on our neighbouring station, so it was arranged he would swing by on his way home and remuster the paddock. His job was easy in the small paddock, but we had to redraft the eight hundred cows we had just released. So instead of drafting 3,200 cattle, we had to draft four thousand animals.

The cows were not happy about being drafted a second time and the crew had a lot of practice climbing the rails to avoid the swishing horns of very agitated cows.

The pressure was also on because we had to get the calves back to their mums. And the delay had us working under lights to catch up on lost time. There were a lot of cows with full udders bellowing from discomfort and a lot of calves bellowing from hunger. Quite a few of the older cows stood against the panels so their calves could squeeze their heads through the rails and have a drink.

With all the cattle drafted, the sale cattle departed in road trains and we moved to the next mustering site. While some of the crew were dismantling yards there was fence building in progress and the new horse yards, under Papa's expert care, were taking shape. The yards no longer consisted of a lot of poles sticking out of the ground. Rails were welded in place and the shape of what was to come was clearly evident.

Even the cattle and horses were sniffing around, curious about the new structure. The yards were built on a rise of land where the animals like to sit at sunrise and sunset, overlooking miles of lower paddocks. It is a favourite spot because there is always a cool breeze coming up from the river. Marlee often leaves a gate of the now-finished yards open. And on a hot day it is not unusual to find the yard full of animals, resting in the shade of the roof and enjoying the breeze.

By mid-September I was thinking maybe we had been a bit ambitious with our plan for the year. We are always anxious to get improvements done and often bite off more than we can chew. With not much of the dry season left, we were bull catching at twenty-two-mile camp. We were also moving the equipment and portable yards into Bull Creek which was a distance of around eighteen miles from the last mustering site and over a very rough road. The road had to be bulldozed and graded in places for the vehicles to get through. Then the chopper mustering, drafting and branding had to take place before everything was moved back to homebase before any rain trapped us in the valley.

Back at the homestead we had to build two large equipment sheds and a hangar before it was too hot.

In between all this activity somewhere, I had my birthday. We were just far too busy for the usual day of rest and my favourite meal, so Marlee presented me with a cold beer and grilled cheese that had a burning candle on top! But it was still a birthday to remember because she told me she was expecting a baby. It was yet to be confirmed by the doctor, but Marlee was sure!

So with this exciting news I was off on my next book tour and had continuous engagements, until the first week of December. So I wasn't going to be much help on the station, but I didn't go out and buy a book for reading in my spare time!

CHAPTER 10

October 1995–
December 1995

O ur final muster of the season out at Bull Creek
was problematic from start to finish. We had not
been into the valley for a few years and the road over
the rocky sections was unpassable. So the road had to
be repaired and graded at the creek crossing and over
sandstone ridges. We also did more fencing and built
part of a permanent yard at the mustering site.

The outlay of money for all these improvements
would be justified by the numbers of yarded sale cattle.
So when we were ready to start mustering Marlee called
the abattoir to book in the cattle a few weeks later. She
was informed they had brought their closing date
forward which meant we now only had seven days to
get our sale cattle to the abattoirs in Katherine.

It was total panic stations. We had to muster, draft,
brand and release the cows, calves and breeding bulls
back into the area. Then we had to truck the sale cattle

back to the main valley near the homestead in time for them to be loaded on the road trains. The road—or lack of road—into the Bull Creek valley meant that the road train rigs had no hope of getting in there.

Another major problem was that we had pulled down our old wooden yards back at the homestead and were in the process of building new steel ones. So there was a bit of a juggling act because we only had portable yards to work with. This meant we had to draft and release the cows, calves and breeding bulls out at Bull Creek then dismantle the panels of the empty pens and rush them back to the home yard site. Then they were reassembled before the cattle in the truck arrived from Bull Creek. It was fortunate we only had to do this for one muster as it was a very stressful operation. Timing was crucial and there was no room for breakdowns or hold-ups of any kind.

When the first truckload of cattle was leaving Bull Creek valley there was a tremendous storm in the main valley area near the homestead and inches of rain fell in a few hours. The road from Bull Creek to the yards was through Nutwood and Desert Paddocks. Moments before we reached these paddocks, Franz had been battling bulldust and sand which would bog him down to the axles if he didn't drive on different ground each time. Then he found himself in a sea of mud, hopelessly bogged on the black soil plain.

He was just three-quarters of a mile from the yards with a truckload of very wild cattle. Some of these cattle had just set eyes on a human for the first time in their short lives. There was no chance of jumping them off

the truck and using horses to walk them the short distance to the yards. If we opened the door of the truck
they would be gone faster than Eleisha's sore-eared
mickey.

The only good thing was it was late at night so at
least it was cool for the cattle. But we still had to move
quickly. The problem had to be solved before the re-
appearance of the sun and the heat of the day. There
was no way across the black soil flat: it was just a stretch
of unnavigable goo. The only answer was to build
another road back along the edge of the mountain range,
following the rocky ground until opposite the yards,
then turning right towards the yard site, cutting through
a few fences on the way.

The next problem was that the bulldozer was back at
Bull Creek where it had been building roads, clearing
fence lines and an airstrip. Luckily Franz was not alone.
There was a small convoy travelling behind the cattle
truck—Marlee driving the grader and Gail and Eleisha
in the Toyota. The grader was travelling with the truck
to pull it through the creek crossing or out of bulldust
bogs. But the whole truck down to its axles in the black
soil bog proved a little too much for the grader so the
only answer was to go back and get the bulldozer.

Franz, Marlee and the two girls drove back to the
camp, where Franz swapped the Toyota for the bulldozer. While it took about twenty minutes to cover the
distance in a four-wheel drive, Marlee knew it would
be a slow journey for Franz so she and the girls grabbed
a few hours' sleep.

Franz also had a few short, unintentional snoozes—

165

on the road! But that was understandable as the D8
bulldozer moves at about four miles per hour in good
conditions but this was at night with no lights through
rocky ravines and over sandstone mountain ridges. So
the speed sometimes got down to two miles per hour.
It was a good four hours before he arrived back at the
bogged truck. Franz had been awake for almost twenty-
four hours by this time, but his few catnaps on the
laboriously slow journey did help.

There was no moon that night and by the time
Marlee and the girls turned up at the bogged truck after
a refreshing few hours' sleep there was no sign of Franz
or the bulldozer. They hadn't passed him on the only
road out of Bull Creek so it was obvious he had gone
off the track. Marlee turned off the engine and heard
the sound of the dear old dozer. Franz was heading
slightly bush so Marlee flashed the lights of the utility in
the direction of the noise. Almost immediately she heard
a change in the engine revs as Franz changed the direction of our old faithful forty-six-tonne machine.

When the bulldozer finally trundled out of the dark-
ness and stopped at the edge of the bog, her journey
was far from complete. The truck had to be pulled out
of its muddy resting place and taken to the yards.

Franz swapped the bulldozer for the wheel of the
bogged truck and Marlee handed the utility over to
Eleisha and Gail and climbed up onto the dozer. The
girls continued onto the homestead but they too got
bogged further down the road and had to walk the rest
of the way home.

It was a very busy night out on the flat and I'm sure

the cattle and wild animals had a very entertaining time with vehicles getting bogged, people walking, shouting, swearing and the distinctive clunk, clunk, clunk of the bulldozer echoing through the valley.

The roar of the mighty engine sounded across the valley as the dozer effortlessly pulled the cattle truck out of the sea of congealed mud in a matter of minutes. With Marlee driving, the dozer slowly moved through the bush and cleared the way for the truck along the foot of the mountain range, sticking to the rocky hard country and skirting the black soil. In a few places trees had to be cleared because there was nowhere else to go, but being very conscious of every one of our trees, Marlee usually found a way through and saved the tree.

Sunrise made the job much easier and their speed increased. They had to cut through two paddock fences and arrived at the yards by midmorning. The cattle were happy to see the ground and have room to move, even if they were in the yards. Water and hay made them even more content.

It was a busy road to Bull Creek the first few weeks of October. There wasn't much sleep as we had 350 cattle to get to the meatworks before they closed in seven days. If we didn't get them up to the main yard site in time to meet the road trains then they would all have to be let go until next year. A lot of money had been outlayed to get to this point, so failure was not an option.

Even the girl cooking was experiencing weird hours, often serving dinner at midnight to various groups and sometimes seeing no-one back at the homestead for the entire day.

The main objective was achieved and all the cattle were waiting in the yards when the road trains arrived. The cattle were loaded and the big machines moved off, climbing through their many gears, gathering power for the long pull ahead.

There was a collective sigh from the entire crew as they sagged onto the nearest resting place and watched the road trains disappear in clouds of dust.

Days of reclining around the pool and sleeping followed as everyone caught up on much-needed rest. But it was soon back to work. The last of the yard at Bull Creek had to be brought back and the mustering site had to be cleared.

After a day of packing, a safari train consisting of the front-end loader, grader, portable loading ramp, trailers, trucks and Toyotas with steel portable panels, camp-site equipment and tools moved slowly out of the valley.

The same day the crew moved into Bull Creek for the last muster of the season, I left on tour for *Some of My Friends Have Tails*. I got daily reports on their progress as I travelled around Australia, starting in Perth on the 2nd October. The book tour was combined with the Breast Screen breast cancer awareness campaign. The advertising campaign had started back in February while I was in South Africa and was going very well. The month after it was launched on television and in all print media, there were fifty thousand bookings in one month. I find this a staggering figure and am very proud that I had something to do with it.

When I first saw the Breast Screen commercials they didn't seem out of the ordinary to me. Everyone connected with them seemed pleased, but I don't think even they expected such a huge response. I certainly didn't. But maybe I was too busy being thankful I didn't look like a beetroot! And was marvelling how the photographer made me look, well, normal.

Before I appeared in these ads when I went shopping, perhaps a few people would recognise me because they had read my books. A few months after the ads came out I was recognised everywhere.

A lot of men, mind you, didn't know my name, and I got remarks like, 'You're that sheila from the bush, aren't you?'

But my favourite comment came from a taxi driver in Sydney. He was driving me out to Mascot for the 7 a.m. flight to Darwin. A few times during the journey I saw him looking at me in the rear-vision mirror then shaking his head and mumbling to himself. As he was taking my luggage out of the car he asked, 'Goin' far?'

'Yes I'm off home to Darwin.'

He paused and looked closely at me, then put down the suitcase and jabbed an index finger in my direction. 'I know you now, you're that sheila in the boobs ads!'

I was trying to think up a suitable reply but wasn't having much luck so early in the morning.

Then he continued, 'Yeh, I told me missus, "'ere listen to this sheila. She's from the bush so she's dinkum, and whatever it is she's selling go get it, 'cause it's free".'

He tipped his finger to his head in a mock salute, told me to keep up the good work and got into his cab and drove away.

I received this letter from a delightful woman in her eighties.

'When you started appearing on the telly in every break telling me, "if I haven't, well I bloody well should!" well, I turned you down to start with, because I don't approve of swearing. But it didn't do any good because you were there and I could lip-read so I still could hear you in my brain. So I finally said, "All right, all right! I'll go!"'

On her next visit to her doctor she mentioned that maybe she should have a mammogram. He told her she really didn't have to bother as she was too old.

But when she turned on the television there I was telling her, 'you owe it to yourself no matter what age you are.'

So she called the number on the screen and they told her she should come for a test. She booked in, had a mammogram and was shocked to learn she had breast cancer. It was in the early stages and she only lost one breast and two years down the track she is still clear and enjoying life. My first thought was she should change her doctor!

The ad even convinced my sister to have a mammogram. She informed me she had to do it because she was my sister and how would it look if she was asked if she'd had a mammogram and couldn't say, 'Yes'. This was something I hadn't even thought about, but on reflection she was perfectly right.

I hadn't worried about the mammogram I had at the beginning of the campaign. But during the following two years I met and heard so many stories about this disease I certainly thought a lot more about breast cancer. Knowing now, it strikes anywhere, I went for my second x-ray with a great deal more awareness, trying to visualise how I would react if the news was not good.

When I returned home a week later I sat down and went through my messages. In the middle of the long list of callers, one message stood out: 'Please call the Breast Screen Clinic in Darwin, urgently'.

The words jumped off the page and hit me first in the throat, then the chest and stomach. It was minutes before I could compose myself enough to breath normally and phone the clinic. The phone rang out as it was after hours on a Friday afternoon and I realised I had a whole weekend to get through, not knowing what my results were.

I made a decision not to tell Marlee, as she was pregnant, and I didn't want to worry her. So I tried to busy myself with tasks that would take my mind off it, but all I could think about was the worst possible outcome. Marlee could tell I was not myself and spent the whole weekend asking me if I was okay.

When I finally got in contact with the clinic on Monday morning they thanked me for calling back and said that they were wondering if the clinic could get permission to use my posters at an upcoming function!

Relief coursed through my body as I tried to sound normal and gave an elated 'yes' in reply.

Those two days gave me just a tiny glimpse of what it is like for the women who are dealt this terible blow and I know from Marlee's experience just what it is like for the families of people with cancer. I take my hat off to anyone who has to deal with any cancer, you are the bravest of the brave.

I arrived back at the station on the 31st October a little tired. But the hard work of the prolonged tour had been worth it. *Some of My Friends Have Tails* went onto the bestseller list in seven days, reaching number one and staying on the list for a few months. It was also joined on the list by *From Strength to Strength* for a short period of time.

The station was a hive of activity and the equipment sheds were finished. Jim Coggan (from whom we bought the sheds) and his wife, Pauline, had arrived on the property while I was on tour. Jim had directed and worked with Franz and the team and the sheds went up in record time. I'm sure Jim was pleasantly surprised when he found all the foundation footings for the sheds were level and in line. I don't think he counted on a perfectionist such as our Franz in the middle of the Outback. He complimented Franz, saying he had never seen anyone work as hard as he did. Pauline was roped into cooking and was a terrific help . . . and a good cook!

It was a mammoth job well done. And it brought the usual surprises. One of our stockmen who couldn't walk on flat ground without falling over his feet, was like a cat thirty feet up in the air, walking on a six-inch girder on the roof of the hangar. You never can tell!

The sheds and the hangar are superb. Franz immediately parked all the equipment in the shed bays and wheeled the little plane into her new home in the vast expanse of the hangar.

It took a while to get used to having these new sheds. Drew, our farmer–stockman from New Zealand, went to Katherine one day to pick up a load of wet season supplies and was due home about ten o'clock that night.

The next morning Franz looked out and saw the truck wasn't parked at the back gate and assumed Drew had broken down on the road or was bogged in one of the creeks. So after a quick bite to eat he was off down the road to look for our lost truck.

Half an hour later Drew walked in the door of the homestead and Marlee asked him where Franz was. Drew looked puzzled and replied he didn't know. Franz got home five hours later!

Drew had arrived home at ten o'clock the night before and had parked the loaded truck in the new equipment shed because it looked like rain and he didn't want the load to get wet.

After a five-hour drive to the front gate and back Franz never again forgot to look in the sheds whenever a vehicle was overdue.

The year was finally slowing down. November was blissful—apart from the everyday work on the station, opening mountains of mail, swimming through a sea of office work and a few trips to conferences, I was home all month!

My book of quotes, *Outback Wisdom*, was launched and hit the bestseller lists and before I knew it, December had arrived. Marlee and I had a few days in Darwin shopping for Christmas. Marlee had another clean test for cancer behind her and was trying to come to terms with her growing stomach. She was lucky though, and carried like me—not all out in front—so at six months did not look too bad at all. One male friend in Darwin didn't even know she was pregnant and in typical male fashion said he thought, 'She had stacked a bit on'!

Marlee terrified her gynaecologist with what she was doing during her pregnancy. He repeatedly requested she give up things like horse mustering, bullcatching and castrating seeing she was now approaching the latter part of her pregnancy. I wondered what he would have to say about her leaping over steel panels in cattle yards, rushing to the rescue of Eleisha and facing a wild bull in the process. But she was only a few months pregnant then and she now admitted her stomach was getting in the way when she was working, much to his relief. But then she had him back in panic mode when she said she would like to go for her helicopter licence during the next spare few months! He explained that this was not the thing to occupy the last months of a pregnancy and could she do something else like reading or painting.

Marlee promised him she would slow down, but he

was worried about Marlee's definition of slow down. But she did listen ... and went ploughing.

December was busy with ploughing and planting hay. We had the crop planted before the end of December which was unusual, but possible because of the early heavy rains in November and December. All the staff left at various stages during the month. And Cupid had struck again. So we had another starry-eyed couple wandering off into the sunset holding hands.

Christmas Day was quiet and enjoyable. It was the first time we had stopped during the year to take stock of all our work. The fact that we had achieved all we had planned for the year made it a very enjoyable pause. And this had all been made possible because we had a good team.

And so yet another year was at an end. Marlee and Franz went to sleep early on New Year's Eve and I again found myself sitting out under the stars, sipping cold beer out of a champagne goblet, with the dogs faithfully at my side. Boots joined us and slurped beer out of my glass while I reminisced. I let him continue to make a mess of the glass and I drank from the bottle.

I finished the year with the thought I think passes through most of our minds at this time, 'I wonder what the hell life will throw at me this year!'

CHAPTER 11

January 1996–
June 1996

The first entry in my new diary was, 'Home all January! Yahoo!'

We started the year in style, eating wild duck for dinner on New Year's Day. The next day was Danielle's birthday. I arranged for flowers to be delivered to her and as usual told her a birthday present would be sent just as soon as one of us got to a shop and could buy her a gift.

Our sorghum crop was growing nicely, so there were constant cocky patrols to discourage them from pulling the entire crop of seedlings out of the ground. With the good rains that were falling we were confident the patrols would not be for much longer as the crop would soon be at what we call, 'Can't take-off height'. This is when the plants are about ten-inches tall and the cocka-toos don't land because they have no room for take-off. We waited eagerly for the approach of the end of cocky patrol, but knew they would be back as soon as the crop developed heads of seeds.

Franz was working on the roof over the new round horse yards. We had no cook. Again! So Marlee was cooking in between building a small paddock for the stallion off the new horse yards. I was, as usual, writing.

As the roof over the horse yard took shape Marlee was also mustering and drafting horses—against doctor's orders—but she assured me the horses had already been handled and were quiet. She said she was just advancing their training and that Franz would be there with her.

Marlee and I flew to Darwin for her doctor's appointment. She was now having trouble reaching the control pedals due to her growing tummy and decided she would not fly again until after the birth of the baby.

After the doctor declared all was well we didn't have enough light left to fly back to the station, so we stayed in town and went to a movie together. It had been years since we'd done that.

On the flight home the plane started to vibrate strangely which had our adrenalin pumping for the rest of the journey. All gauges were registering normal, so we had no idea of the cause. The engine didn't miss a beat nor did we notice any change in the power. We were flying over some extremely isolated country, and really didn't have an option to go anywhere but on to Bullo where we landed safely.

Franz had many long phone conversations with an aircraft engineer and the vibration was put down to worn engine mountings. On inspection in Darwin this was confirmed and after they were replaced the plane behaved herself again.

The wet season was not following the usual pattern. Dust storms continued well into January, indicating not enough soaking rain had fallen to keep the soil together. We would watch dark clouds approaching, and wait hopefully for rain, but instead we had violent dry dust storms which dumped tonnes of dirt into the valley, leaving everything covered in dust.

The sorghum crop was visibly wilting—it needed some rain and soon. Hot days indicated rain was close by. And we prayed it would rain. Of course we had a fair chance of this prayer being answered as we were in the middle of the rainy season and storms were surrounding the valley.

It was only a matter of time before we had an amazing electric storm with only a bit of rain, but enough to water the crop. This was followed a week later by good soaking rain that came into the valley ahead of a cyclonic low hovering off the Western Australian coast.

Between rain storms we took delivery of a brand new tractor. The salesman must have been very keen to make this sale because he braved our road and brought the tractor in on a small truck in the middle of the wet season. It hadn't been planned that way. The American factory was late with the delivery and being American,

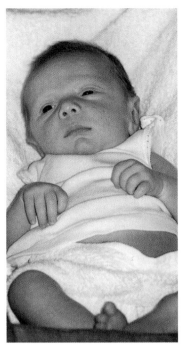

Ben at five weeks of age.

Ben with his dad, Uncle Robert (Franz's brother) and his first Barra.

Ground check for spot fires after the Auvergne Station fire.

Marlee, Ben, me, Danielle and Natalie.

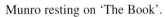

Eleisha Thompson and Munro, as a puppy.

Munro resting on 'The Book'.

Jack Thompson talking about his love of the Territory at the launch of Billy Thorpe's book *Sex and Thugs and Rock'n'Roll.*

Family and friends on 'This Is Your Life'.

Ben wasn't so sure what to do with birthday cake no.1, but he had no problems with no.2.

Ben on the bull catcher, ready for work.

Giant Bottle tree.

Tourists on the 'Bullo River sightseeing bus'.

Bullo then.

Bullo now, with new roof and pool fence.

The birdbath in foreground.

The Finch decided we were friendlier than mother nature, so she built her nest in our indoor pot plant.

Bird nest with babies.

Birds are not the only wildlife we find indoors. Five frogs and a soup ladle.

Munro helping me to
sort through the mail
that survived the
Katherine floods.

The helicopter pushed
these cattle off an island,
created by flooded rivers
and creeks, to higher land.

Thankfully the house
and airstrip were high . . .
but not dry.

they had no concept of the wet season cutting off our road for five months at a time. But the Darwin representative knew we needed the tractor and was willing to take the chance and come in our road. He had a few hairy moments going around some of the major washouts on the jump-ups, but apart from that he said the road was fairly good.

We looked at the tractor sitting in all its glory. A brand new, beautiful, gleaming tractor with the latest in modern technology. Hydraulics everywhere including a hydraulic seat, a dashboard that resembled a jet aircraft's, air-conditioning, radio, CD player, the list goes on . . .

We certainly have come a long way tractor-wise. I can still see Diesel Don, Uncle Dick's faithful assistant mechanic, back in the early seventies, slashing the airstrip on our old red tractor. The seat was welded to a massive steel spring—I have strong suspicions this spring was an Uncle Dick modification, quickly devised when Charlie demanded Dick service the tractor because he was going to mow the airstrip. The tractor seat was Dick's subtle revenge, but it backfired because Charlie handed over the mowing job to poor old Diesel Don. Every time Don hit a bump he was airborne, with only the steering wheel to keep him on the tractor. On rough ground he was in the air a good part of the time.

I didn't see Marlee and Franz for the next week, except when they passed the house in the new green machine. Suddenly every job seemed to need the tractor!

THE STRENGTH OF OUR DREAMS

The end of January saw one cyclone move away from the valley and out to sea and another one come right in on its tail. Now the road was definitely closed for the season. The sorghum was now too high for the cocka-toos to take-off so the cocky patrol was discontinued until later in the season.

Franz was busy studying for his chopper licence and Marlee was still discovering all the amazing things the new tractor could do. We also had a new cook in Kununurra waiting for a break in the weather so Franz could fly the short trip to pick her up.

It was raining daily and the grass grew as you watched it. Our old slasher was having trouble keeping up with just the airstrip and the grass in the garden was two-feet high. The slasher was in danger of rattling itself apart. It is so old the bolts slip through the bolt holes. To give some indication of its age we paid around eight hundred dollars for it when we bought it new. The replacement equivalent today would be $5,500. Franz packed the holes hoping it would stay together for a few more years. Marlee presented a strange sight as she headed out to slash the airstrip—a beautiful new tractor towing our very old, worn-out slasher. Fingers were crossed it would last to slash the airstrip, in between the storms, to keep the grass down so the mail plane—which hadn't been able to land the previous week—could land, if it ever turned up.

The weather deteriorated more each day and gale-force winds were reported along the coast from Darwin down to Bullo and into Western Australia. I was due to fly out of Bullo to a conference in Sydney and straight onto the Gold Coast to a conference at Jupiter's. Franz was able to fly me to Darwin to catch the plane south but it was another of those hair-raising flights down close to the ground the whole way.

When I returned the still very new cook was having trouble coping with the heat, which was understandable, as January and February have to be the hottest months of the year, with temperatures consistently in the high thirties, and edging regularly into the forties. Franz was suffering very badly with hayfever so he went to Darwin to see the doctor and Marlee went for her next baby appointment. The doctor said she was doing well, which seemed to amaze him when she told him what she did.

The cook decided to leave! This didn't surprise anyone except the cook. So I came out of my writing hole to help Marlee with the cooking and cleaning.

I started by tackling the storeroom which was sadly in need of attention. I restacked the large steel shelves and stood back to admire my work. The shelves groaned and twisted into an unusual shape, spilling the contents in a heap at my feet. After repairing the shelves, I restacked them. I decided my time was put to better use writing, so I left the house to Marlee and went back to work.

Franz took the cook to town and we started looking for the next one.

Our next visitors were representatives of a bus company who wanted to bring busloads of tourists into the station for the day on a weekly basis from May to the end of the year. Thirty-five people per bus and sometimes two buses per week represented a lot of work. Not even mentioning the nightmares of the road with buses getting bogged or breaking down. I could see us running a full-time towing service.

So as good as the regular income would have been, I had to say no, we were too busy and couldn't manage it at present. Quality of life has to figure somewhere in this constant struggle to survive and I could see this venture could decrease my quality of life in one fell swoop.

I had visions of no cook, Marlee or the baby sick and me in the kitchen cooking for forty people and finding a bed for a busload of people if they couldn't get out. No, I was getting too old for this type of superhuman effort.

A new cook arrived and left a few days later, justifying my 'no buses' decision.

Every now and then someone comes along and you just know a guardian angel has sent them. Our quest for a mechanic was up there with finding a cook and I'd decided both were as likely as finding the Golden Fleece. But we received a letter from a retired engineer who said he'd like to come to Bullo and help us with some of our many projects.

Marlee spoke to him on the phone and he sounded very nice. And he didn't drink! So Marlee said he should come for a few weeks and we would see what happened after that.

182

When Alan arrived we worried about his age and the effect the heat would have on him. I told Franz not to even ask him to lift a spanner, so afraid was I of him collapsing. He just seemed too frail for the Outback.

But Alan quietly went about his work, and it wasn't long before he looked like a different man—tanned and quite spritely. I had thought he wouldn't last a week, but it turned out he was here for ten months. He was a help in every domain, even the kitchen where he would step in and cook a meal when Marlee and I had our hands full. Alan always kept the kitchen tidy and there was never any fuss over producing the meal—unlike some of the hired cooks.

This angel in disguise was also a great help to Franz with the building of our new cattle yards. Without Alan's quiet, consistent back-up, I don't think Franz could have finished in time for the beginning of mustering season. Of course we had some young men for the heavy work of cementing in posts and carrying the steel, but Alan provided expertise and guidance to the workers that was invaluable. Franz could go off on another job when needed and Alan would oversee the men working on the yards.

No matter what you needed, Alan was there. He was helpful in every way—even down to opening the aeroplane gate and hangar door when the plane came home. The aeroplane gate was not a small thing, it was a section of the fence that could be pulled aside to allow the plane to taxi into the garden, sort of an oversized 'cocky's gate'. Yes, I have no doubt my guardian angels sent Alan.

183

Because of the unpredictable weather at the beginning of each year and not being too thrilled about flying at five-hundred feet all the way to Darwin, I had learned not to take bookings in the first three months of the year. Yet when I looked at my diary, for some reason I had accepted quite a few bookings in these months. The year just didn't have enough months in it for me to do all I needed to! Because my books were so popular I found myself travelling a great deal and it was now getting to the point where I didn't have time to write them! The wet season was the only time I had to write and now speaking and travelling were infringing into this territory.

So my writing suffered this wet season. But I have to say my concentration was lacking for other reasons and I finally gave up trying to write until this event was over. The excitement of the approaching birth of Marlee's baby was occupying most of my thoughts.

Franz and Marlee came to Darwin to pick me up after a conference and Marlee had another check-up. The ultrasound confirmed the baby was a boy. This was very exciting news as we had had such a long run of girls, and it would be nice to have a boy in there somewhere. He was certainly going to have a lot of female cousins.

The doctor said Marlee had about six weeks to go and told her to take it fairly easy. This statement usually went over Marlee's head, just as it did this time. A lot can be done in six weeks.

Franz was off to Caloundra to stay with Susan and Ralph and do the flying part for his commercial chopper licence. After a careful study of the year's work ahead, he realised if he wanted to get the flying in, it would have to be then or in twelve months' time.

I was going to Sydney at the same time so we left a very pregnant Marlee in charge of the station assisted by Alan. I prayed the doctor was right and she still had six weeks to go. But both Franz and Marlee told me I worry too much and Marlee did not seem the least bit nervous that Franz was away from the station. I flew back home after three days by charter plane as Marlee could definitely not reach the control pedals on the plane anymore and that is a definite disadvantage when flying!

Marlee was busy working and talked to Franz on the phone daily, who was building up his hours at a very fast rate and assured her he would be home in plenty of time for the arrival of the baby. I have to say I didn't sleep much at night, ready for Marlee to burst into my room and say the words, 'It has started!' But as Marlee and Franz say, I worry too much.

Franz passed his commercial licence and when he arrived home on the 30th March, he told us we now had to call him Captain Ranacher! Mr Mustang, his dog, howled for half an hour without pause. There was no way we could shut him up. Every time he looked at Franz he would launch into a painful rendition of howls of happiness.

Maybe he was trying to tell Franz we tried to do away with him while he was away. Mr Mustang is a funny dog, so devoted to Franz he is jealous of Marlee. While Franz was away Marlee decided to try and cure

Mustang's skin itch. She read up on the subject in one of the animal medical books and in some natural healing books and came up with a mixture of herbs and oils to soak him in daily.

Marlee filled the bath in the old brown bathroom and took him in to soak him in a lovely perfumed bath. The look of doom on his face sent her into peals of laughter. I rushed in to see what was happening, praying it was not the beginning of labour pains. Marlee pointed to Mustang and the look on his face was so expressive I too burst into laughter. He could not have been more fatalistic if he were standing in front of a guillotine. I am sure he thought Marlee was about to do him in! His head hung almost to the ground and he looked up with most of the whites of his eyes showing.

We coaxed him into the bath, and not without a lot of pulling on my behalf. He wrapped his claws over the side of the bath and I had to peel them off to finally get him in the water.

After he accepted we were not going to drown him, he ended up enjoying himself. So much so that by the end of the week he was bounding into the bathroom and leaping into his daily therapeutic bath with glee.

He even started wagging his tail when he greeted Marlee which was a major breakthrough. However, after the howling welcome to Franz he returned to his grumpy self again. He became very possessive of Franz once more and was in constant competition with Marlee for Franz's affection.

Marlee was now due in two weeks but could give birth any day. By this time I was extremely nervous and had visions of Franz and myself presiding over the birth! Marlee had a few jobs she wanted to complete before she left, but I put my foot down and said I wanted to go to town, *now!* But it was another week before my daily pleadings got the both of them down and we finally packed and flew to Darwin to await the baby's birth.

During that week Franz started to demolish the old staff sleeping quarters, which meant we were committed to building the new ones as there would soon be nowhere for anyone to sleep. And Marlee had spent her time in the air-conditioned tractor harvesting the sorghum.

Franz flew back home the morning after flying us to Darwin with a new cook and housekeeper. Marlee and I both hoped the house would be clean when we arrived home with the new baby. Meanwhile we settled into the apartment where we were staying and Franz spoke to us daily. A low had moved in over the station so they had stopped mowing the sorghum and Franz was sure that by working through the night he could bale what had already been mown so we would not lose any hay. We listened with interest to the progress of the work at the station, but had to admit we were preoccupied with the birth of the baby, not the station.

Marlee and my first urgent task was to go and buy some clothes for the baby. I had bought some coloured nappies I couldn't resist and a few sleeping outfits in Sydney, but other than this the little baby had nothing ready for his birth. But we were going to change all that in the next week. Or so we thought.

187

After a good breakfast on the first day we attacked the shops. Neither of us could remember the last time we had a week to go shopping together. By lunchtime Marlee was tired, so we went to our favourite restaurant to have a light meal and to sit in the cool of the air-conditioning.

After an hour Marlee still didn't feel any better so we went back to the apartment. I called the doctor and after a long conversation, he wanted to see her. The result of his examination was to put her straight into hospital. I was stunned! Marlee's blood pressure was on the rise and he was worried about pre-eclampsia toxaemia and wanted to keep her under observation.

I had never heard of this problem, but soon learned a lot more about it. You are more susceptible to this problem appearing at any stage in your pregnancy if you are in your thirties and it is your first pregnancy; if you are under five feet three inches tall; and if you suffer migraines. Marlee was all of these, she was so lucky it only appeared in the last week of her pregnancy.

The next morning her blood pressure had not settled and the doctor wanted to bring on the baby. He explained that if her blood pressure went too high it would be life threatening for the baby and if she went onto drugs to control its rise, this would be bad for both of them. If they couldn't control the blood pressure and it went too high Marlee could lapse into a coma! I was sick to the stomach.

I called Franz and told him to fly to Darwin immediately. Weather had closed in over Bullo, but Franz managed to fly low up the Victoria River and follow the coastline all the way to Darwin. He came straight to the hospital and the three of us listened to the doctor explain the situation that had suddenly appeared and what the alternatives were for Marlee and Franz and their baby.

Marlee had been looking forward to a natural birth but this was something you didn't fool with, so the doctor started procedures to induce the baby's birth. If everything went according to plan Marlee would have the baby in the next twenty-four hours.

Way back when she first told me she was pregnant and the baby was due in April, I didn't take any more bookings for the month. However there had already been one booking on the 13th April which I was leaving for on the 12th. I jokingly said all through the pregnancy that would be when the baby arrived. However the doctor assured me the baby would be born before that.

The baby did not arrive when he was supposed to or all the next day and Franz and I sat watching Marlee's every move. Sure enough, the next afternoon when I was walking out the door to go to the airport, Marlee's water broke. So I left her with Franz and headed for Perth.

My heart and soul were in that delivery room with Marlee on the long flight to Perth. I landed in Perth at fifteen minutes to midnight and baby Ben touched down in Darwin at the same time!

Marlee did not have an easy time. Ben's head was very large and she was having great difficulty with the birth. The doctor was very patient and told her to take her time. Everything changed when a pregnant woman was

189

rushed into the hospital haemorrhaging and needing an emergency caesarean. Marlee's doctor was the only doctor on duty so he found himself with two women having difficulties. The doctor told Marlee she was also close to having a caesarean if she didn't give birth soon. This prospect upset Marlee so much her next few pushes were so hard she cracked her tailbone and she too started haemorrhaging!

Franz was completely calm and helpful throughout the entire drama. Marlee said it was just as well I was not there because the room was awash with blood. I just know I would have passed out in the middle of it all.

I called at midnight as soon as I touched down, not knowing Marlee was in the midst of this emergency. The doctor was stabilising Marlee's haemorrhaging then rushing to operate on the woman in the next room. Franz was assisting the male nurse with Marlee then the paediatrician with the baby. It must have been quite a scene, yet when Franz answered my phone call his voice was as calm as could be. He just said the baby had been born and that they were a bit busy and he would call me when I reached the hotel.

Franz called me at my hotel to tell me I had a healthy little grandson. But he was not so little—Ben was quite a long baby. When I asked about Marlee he said she was well. That was stretching the truth a bit, but Marlee told him not to say anything to worry me. When I asked Franz if he was OK, his only complaint was he had blisters on his fingertips from massaging Marlee's back and shoulders for a day and a half!

When I arrived back at the hospital two days later,

Marlee looked very tired and was in quite a bit of pain from the cracked bone. Her bruised bladder was still not working properly and her blood pressure was still fairly high. The joys of motherhood!

When I looked at my grandson, it was like looking at a clone of Franz. It was amazing to me that a baby could look so completely like one parent. But when I studied him closely, as all grandmothers do, I could see Marlee's features were also there in his dear little face.

It was a few more days before Marlee started to improve. Her blood pressure started to go down, other parts of her body started working normally and she brightened considerably. Once I was there Franz headed back to the station, where Alan, bless his heart, was holding the fort. He was not only directing the cook and housekeeper, but also the men building in the yard.

When Franz arrived home the cook and domestic gave notice. Those two had only lasted a few days and it probably would not have been that long if the plane had been on Bullo and not in Darwin. Franz and Alan handled this new turn of events with Alan back to chief cook and bottle washer. So Marlee and I didn't know the homestead was without cook and housekeeper and at the mercy of a group of men and we went on enjoying our time in Darwin and our new baby boy.

Flowers and phone calls came from everywhere including Austria. Marlee's room soon resembled a florist so we moved some of the flowers into other parts of the ward.

Franz's family called the hospital when Franz was back at the station. Marlee and I did a lot of 'ja'ing' and when

191

we finished the call we had no idea if they knew if the baby was a boy, let alone any other details. We called Franz and told him to call home, so they were not confused for long.

By the end of the week Marlee was well and truly on the mend and we were ready to take Ben into the outside world. Marlee had been so much calmer than me all the way through this exciting event. About the only time I really was helpful was when I did most of the emergency shopping required, like nappies and sleeping shirts, along with the everyday things that would be needed the first week out of hospital. Ben's wardrobe was taking shape slowly, in fits and starts.

Franz arrived back from the station and told us of the latest departure of the houehold staff . . . over a week ago! And amused us with stories of the all-male crew looking after themselves, everyone taking turns at cooking mainly to get a change from Alan's daily meal of hamburgers and self-saucing chocolate pudding. But at the end of each day they were more than happy to sit down to the same meal. It was always nicely cooked and they were usually tired and appreciated the meal ready and waiting.

But Marlee and I were well aware of what a house full of men could do to the homestead and although we wanted to get home, we knew it was not going to be all shiny and clean! So there was some rushing around Darwin trying to find replacement staff.

The plan was to stay in Darwin one night and fly down to the station next morning early so we would have a smooth flight home. On the way to the apartment from the hospital we stopped at a baby shop to buy a bassinet for Ben's first night out of hospital.

I smiled as I watched Marlee buy the bassinet, remembering back to before Danielle's Natalie was born. Everything a baby would need for the first year was waiting and assembled in the nursery a few days after Danielle knew she was pregnant. I called Danielle when she was only four months pregnant and said I would like to buy something for the new baby and what didn't she have? Well, after a good half an hour conversation it was clear there wasn't a thing the baby would need. So I moved onto the next year and bought a gift for a one-year-old, but didn't ask, because I was sure she already had that year organised too.

Here we were ten days along and just buying Ben's bed. But on his first night out of hospital Ben had clothes and a bed and was surrounded by love. With these essentials, a newborn needs nothing more.

We went home the next morning after Ben and Marlee went for one more check-up with their doctors. Friends in Darwin, Geoff and Kylie, came out to the plane to see us off and took a photo of Ben about to embark on his first plane ride at the age of ten days. He was a perfect traveller and slept all the way home.

Alan gave us a great welcome. I think he was very glad to see us after holding the fort. I took over the cooking for a few days, which pleased him and he took off down to the workshop with Franz, before I changed my mind. Marlee settled into being a mother and Ben just settled.

We hadn't found any household help in Darwin. But the next day Franz flew into Kununurra for a food order and he found another cook. I came back to Kununurra two days later after a speaking engagement and Franz flew me out to the station with yet another set of cook and domestic!

I was home for the next fourteen days and Marlee took the opportunity to start grading the road. She took Ben with her in the grader in the early hours of the morning when it was cool. I just know, without the slightest doubt, that we have the only grader in the world with a baby capsule and a drop-down, plate-steel change. table! Franz laughed at Marlee when she requested these modifications, but when she told him there was nowhere to change Ben and she had to grade the road, he made the alterations.

When Ben wasn't acting as assistant grader driver, I had him for the rest of the day. But these peaceful two weeks of sharing my afternoons with Ben passed too quickly and I was soon off on a three-conference trip. Ben's first nanny was waiting at the airport when I was dropped off and went back to the station with Franz. So Marlee finished grading the road with the nanny and Ben following along behind the grader in the Toyota, ready at hand when he was hungry.

When Franz flew to Darwin a week later to bring me home, Marlee, Ben and the nanny were still grading and had reached the front-gate end of the road, fifty miles away from the homestead. As we approached the

194

valley just on sunset we saw that the whole Pinkerton Mountain range, for at least twenty miles from the Victoria River, was on fire and burning wildly. The most disturbing aspect for us was from our height of a few thousand feet we could see the wind was blowing the fire into the Bullo valley.

Marlee didn't know of the fire, as she'd been out near the highway end of the road, all day. But she soon realised there was a fire close to home. First she smelt smoke and after turning a bend in the road saw that the mountain range as far as she could see was alight.

The wind didn't change overnight, although it did drop a little, and it took up again the next morning with a vengeance. Dawn revealed we were in trouble. The fire was moving down the mountain and showed no chance of abating.

The fire that was about to engulf the valley had been lit by the Bush Fire Council on behalf of Auvernge Station. It was part of the controlled fire burning campaign that is carried out each year. We had decided not to burn, as it was just too dry for our liking. But as I looked out across the mountain range that separated the two properties, it seemed whether we wanted to or not, we were burning. And it looked like quite a lot more of the valley and grassland than we would ever contemplate burning, was about to burn.

Marlee called the manager of Auvernge Station to inform him his burning program was now out of control and heading into our valley and we were in danger of losing all our grass. He came over with some men and the station grader to help us bring the fire under control.

195

Marlee drove out the road to get our grader which was still sitting at the front gate with about a day's work left to be done. But there was no time for that now. She met the Auvernge firefighting team halfway out the road, they continued in the road and started to help Franz who was bulldozing a break to stop the wide front which was now burning near our twenty-two-mile campsite.

When Marlee arrived at our grader she found the fire had swept through the area and burnt around the grader in a complete circle. If she hadn't graded her usual fire circle around it the night before we would have lost the grader.

Marlee arrived at the scene of the firebreak where they had finished the break only to watch the fire jump it effortlessly and roar off down the valley. It was advancing at such a pace everyone had to drop back sixteen miles to clear another firebreak at the six-mile yard site, which is only six miles from the homestead. This time they had the Bullo River and Dingo Creek as backstops on two sides of the break. But if the fire jumped this break, we really would be in trouble. There was nothing in the lower valley to stop it from burning all our best paddocks and all the feed for the rest of the year. So there was no thought of failure. This fire had to be stopped at six-mile because in the middle of all the feed for the rest of the year also sat our homestead. Not to mention all the equipment sheds, staff quarters, our generator shed and all the water-pumping equipment.

So the race was on and even after retreating all those miles, with two graders, the bulldozer and every person on the station working, we barely had the break finished and the back-burning alight before the fire came roaring down the valley to join the back-burning fire.

Everyone watched with relief as the intensity of the fire faded when it crashed into the wall of back-burning. There was an impressive whooshing noise as fire collided with fire. The fire faded as it ran out of fuel, appearing as if an invisible hand had turned down a giant gas jet. Where minutes earlier a great wall of flames had rushed forward devouring everything in its path, there was now a quiet, receding fire. It was still intensive in heat but with no forceful forward power. The fire ran into burnt fuel and quickly dissolved into small sputtering flames, struggling to survive. It appeared the battle had been won. The small fires still burning could be worked on now the fire was not growing bigger by the second.

There was still work ahead, but the break would protect the lower sixteen miles of the valley, our breeding paddocks and the homestead area. Weary people fell into bed, thankful for a night's rest.

During the night winds fanned burning trees and the fire established itself on the other side of the firebreak and was once more heading down the valley for the paddocks and the house. A predawn start had the bulldozer, two graders and every able body working. It took until evening before it looked like we had once more stopped it in its tracks.

Franz went out late at night and drove along the break to make sure the fire was contained only to find the wind had carried this dreaded menace into new unburnt country.

Everyone headed out very early, before light, and started fighting again. It was very rough going this time, out the back of Bullion Paddock along the foot of the mountain range. As this is sandstone country, it was difficult grading any kind of break and fighting the fire on foot was demanding. People and machines had to fight for every inch of ground as the fire wove intricate patterns between trees and sandstone boulders. Treetops and clumps of grass ignited into flames without warning and most of the firefighting was done by hand with wet bags beating the grass in amongst the sandstone boulders. The machines graded breaks and back-burned and kept the fire from branching off into other valleys and spreading back into the main valley on a wide front. It was a hot, exhausting and dangerous day. The next day was more of the same—fighting and containing the fire all day.

The fifth day dawned and Franz went up in the plane to fly over the area. He came back and said the fire was finally out. So our men spent the next few days cleaning up the mess around the paddocks close to the homestead.

Marlee was away so much during these days that when she finally did come home to stay after the fire was beaten, Ben didn't know her at first and wouldn't leave my arms. During the days of around-the-clock firefighting Marlee would race into the house, express milk into bottles and rush out again. Sometimes she couldn't stop grading and Ben had to be content with boiled water with sugar. I made a note during these hectic days to get a stand-by supply of formula milk!

As always, problems seem to follow problems. Marlee was off to Kununurra in the station wagon soon after and along the highway, just outside our gate, the front axle seized. The nut was sheared off on a rock and all the oil leaked out. Marlee, Ben and the nanny were sitting on the side of the road when they were picked up by tourists, who just happened to be book fans! After many photos with Marlee and Ben they dropped them off at Newry Station and Marlee waited for the towtruck to come out from Kununurra.

Ben was all of four weeks old and he had already been in a plane, a grader and now a towtruck. But he seemed to take it all in his stride.

They arrived home at around midnight. It was a long day for a tiny baby and I was worried about putting him through such rigours. I asked Marlee how he fared and she replied wearily as she wandered off to bed with the sleeping Ben in her arms, 'He ate, slept and pooed all day!'

CHAPTER 12

July 1996– December 1996

The next big event in our lives was Bazza, our Bazadaise bull, going to the Katherine Show for the second time. Getting to the show involved a mass of problems. The first problem was we had sold our small truck in December. So to get Bazza to the show we only had our prime mover and a double-decker cattle trailer. We thought it would be a bit over the top to turn up at the show with one bull in a double-decker road train, so Marlee found a single-decker trailer for sale in Batchelor, just outside of Darwin.

Marlee and Franz flew over to inspect the trailer and arranged for the owner to drop it off in Timber Creek, one hundred kilometres from our front gate. The day the trailer arrived Marlee left me with Ben and a day's supply of milk in bottles and left for Timber Creek in the prime mover to pick it up.

There was enough milk to last until six o'clock, so

with her estimated time of arrival being mid-afternoon, we would be OK. Ben finished the last drop of milk at six o'clock and there was still no sign of Marlee. Franz was out working in the lower paddock and I didn't expect him back for at least another hour. I knew that if Marlee had broken down in the first hour along the highway after she left Timber Creek, she would be back in town by now and would have called me. So it was safe to say the truck was somewhere along our road. I had no choice but to wait for Franz as I couldn't go racing around the countryside with a small baby.

Two hours later I had a very hungry baby on my hands. Franz had a rushed meal and shower, while I packed some food for Marlee in an esky and tried to comfort Ben. Franz started out on the road and I mixed yet another boiled water and sugar concoction, hoping Ben would drink it.

Franz was only five miles out the road when he met Marlee driving the prime mover. When they got home she sat feeding a ravenous baby while I fed her dinner and she told her story. The trailer brakes had seized going up the first steep jump-up as she came back in our road. She couldn't stop on the jump-up so by the time the prime mover had hauled the protesting trailer to flat ground, the seized brake drums were on fire. Marlee put out the fire with the fire extinguisher and looked at her options. She quickly realised the brakes needed work back at the workshop so the best thing to do was to leave the trailer and drive home in the prime mover. A glance at her watch told her she still had time up her sleeve before Ben ran out of milk.

However the simple task of disconnecting the trailer was now a major problem and Marlee couldn't get it to unhitch. She couldn't drive home dragging the trailer and she knew I would soon be running out of milk.

To release the trailer you need to pull a lever and the clamps which connect it to a vehicle open, but these clamps were not releasing.

The problem Marlee had was that she had to be in two places at once. She had to pull the lever on one side of the truck and at the same time be on the other side of the truck hitting a long steel bar to encourage the lever to move.

Marlee knew we would come looking for her around sunset. But if she sat down and waited she would not get home until midnight and Ben would be six hours without milk. So not wanting to sit around for the next eight hours, she set about solving the problem.

She tied a rope to the end of the lever and threaded it around some steel on the trailer to get leverage, then went over to the other side of the truck and tied it around her waist. While leaning back on the rope she hit the end of the steel bar resting against the end of the lever on the turntable with a hammer. It took her close to an hour but the clamps finally opened. Marlee drove the prime mover home leaving the trailer on top of the jump-up and arrived home at 8 p.m., not midnight.

Franz and I thought her solution was brilliant. But I suppose when you have been solving problems like these for most of your life, they eventually become easier. The work involved had been hard and when I came back into the room with a cup of tea she and Ben were asleep in the chair.

Early the next day Franz went out on the road with all the tools needed to get the trailer moving and brought it back into the workshop for repair. There wasn't a moment to spare as Marlee had to leave for Katherine to get Bazza to the showground in time for registration.

She would be gone for a few days so there was no way enough milk could be stored. So it was off to the Royal Katherine Show for Ben in a short, one trailer version of a road train at the age of just two months.

Most of the staff went to the show and helped with grooming Bazza. The truck made it to the showground at midnight and Bazza had to be groomed and in the ring by eight the next morning. Much to our excitement he won first prize in the other breeds category for the second year in a row. We also won the Land Care Award for the second time for our work with weed control and pasture improvement.

The next highlight of my life would have to have been when I was appointed to the Board of Council for the Order of Australia in July.

When I was told there would be two meetings a year for the council to sit and review the nominations, I thought this wouldn't take too much of my time and fitted in well as I was in Canberra in the months of February and September for board meetings for the Australian Rural Leadership Foundation.

Before long two very heavy suitcases turned up at the

station with six blue folders the size of Sydney telephone books. When I read the information in the letter in the first case, I knew I was in for a lot more than just attending the two meetings in Canberra. It was clear that I had to not only read four thousand pages of information on the one thousand people nominated for Australia Day honours twice a year but I also needed to have a system by which I could quickly refer to anything I needed to at the meetings.

So the months of July and August were filled with my usual station and travelling workloads, and the rest of the time I could be found with my head in a blue folder, reading. Along with this, I had another new job of taking care of baby Ben when Marlee wanted to do something outside and just couldn't work out how to juggle a baby on one arm while doing it.

To me the most important awards are the OAMs (Medal of the Order of Australia) which are awarded for local and community work. These people are never mentioned by the media, which is a shame, as it does the soul good to read about these wonderful people who devote their lives to helping others. So if you have received an OAM for your service to your local community, hold your head high as you are the most important part of the fabric of a strong society and a truly wonderful human being.

A few more cooks arrived and left and I went to a conference for a mining company. I spoke at the closing event, a lunch that wives also attended.

After my speech I was talking to people and signing books when a woman came up to me and said she had just won a lot of money on a bet. She went on to tell me that she had bet her husband that he would enjoy listening to me speak as she had read my books. His reply was, 'What would a woman talking about raising cows on a farm have anything to say that I would remotely be interested in!'

So they made the bet and he had to bring her to the luncheon, which was what she had wanted all along.

The woman said she could see her husband was interested in what I had to say from very early on in the speech but was waiting for him to deny he'd enjoyed the talk. However when I finished he turned to her and said, 'Well, you won that bet!'

After a few more conferences I arrived home to a fax from James listing the top books of the year and I had two in the Australian top ten and three in the adult non-fiction list! Pan Macmillan South Africa also wanted to buy *The Strength In Us All*. I didn't think I could survive another tour so it was decided I would do some newspaper interviews by phone and some radio link-ups.

This was how I found myself back on the three-hour Sunday night religious talkback show. Only this time instead of it being nine o'clock at night, with the time difference I found myself sitting up in my office at four o'clock in the morning. I thought I would just say hello and talk for ten minutes then speak about the second book. But no ... here I was back having a chat with the 'What can I do with my life?' people for the next three hours! I went back to bed at 7 a.m. and slept until lunchtime.

On the 15th August I received a phone call to tell me Charlie's mother had died in America at the age of 105. She would have been 106 in November. I thought about the amazing changes she would have seen over her lifetime.

The season was shaping up to be a bad one for snakes. They were coming into the house far too often and there were a few close calls with king browns.

I was sitting watching the news on television one evening and Sumie was lying on the floor next to my chair. Suddenly Sumie was standing, stock still, staring across the room. I followed her gaze and saw a king brown heading straight for us. I jumped onto the chair and told Sumie to do the same which she did without a second's hesitation.

I called out to Marlee to get the shotgun and threw a magazine at the snake to discourage it from its path which was towards our chair.

It changed course just as Marlee appeared and seconds later it was minus a head. Sumie was congratulated for being so alert and received a large piece of chocolate cake. Then she promptly went looking for more snakes.

———

I was feeling fairly weary by September and Danielle took me to the Hyatt Coolum for my birthday and we had a week of rest. I had a wonderful time—we played tennis and Danielle arranged beauty treatments and massages for me each day.

We had long walks and were able for the first time in years to just talk. And I had uninterrupted time to spend with Natalie. By the end of the week I felt on top of the world. Which was fortunate because the next two and a half months held nonstop work and travel.

James was off to the Frankfurt Book Fair and he'd said to me many times over the years that if we were going to get my first book into America the deal would probably be done in Frankfurt. It was now four years since my first book had been published and the American publishers still had not expressed interest in the book. I thought that maybe if I went to the Fair and met some of them, things might change. James thought it was a good idea and so I made arrangements and booked my ticket to Frankfurt. Marlee had always been at me to go to the Frankfurt Book Fair, so I was puzzled by her strange look when I walked into the kitchen and told her I was going there on the 1st October.

I didn't have too much time to ponder her strange reaction as I was off travelling again. I had two weeks doing the rounds of conferences and directors' meetings and was finishing up in Sydney ready to leave for Frankfurt.

When I reached Sydney I had two days to spare. I

arrived back at the hotel one afternoon to find a message saying James had called and would call again that evening. He was in Scotland and was going to meet me in Frankfurt and I had excited thoughts about an American deal on my book already done.

But when he called it was just to tell me he was delayed in Scotland so could I change my booking and leave a day later.

Jane, my publicist, called and said she had arranged a meeting with the people who were working with us to produce a cookbook and she wanted me to meet them while I was in town. The meeting was arranged for 6 p.m. after which we would all go out to dinner before I left for Germany the next day.

I called the station to talk to Marlee and Alan told me she was down in the breeder paddock. So I went shopping. I was strolling around David Jones' lingerie floor, when I looked up and saw Marlee. You can imagine my surprise and for seconds I just stared, too shocked to say anything. I finally got out a weak, 'Marlee, but . . . but . . .'

'Hi, Mum!'

'What do you mean, "Hi, Mum"? What on earth are you doing here in Sydney?'

'Well I didn't expect to run into you, but the family are having a surprise party for you this evening so now the cat is out of the bag. You will just have to pretend you don't know anything about it and be really surprised tonight.'

Just as she finished this explanation Danielle walked by. She had Natalie with her and was with two of my nieces, so we had a great family reunion in the middle of David Jones.

We eventually went our separate ways and it took me most of the day to get over the amazing turn of events— meeting both my daughters within a few minutes of each other in downtown Sydney.

Jane and Jeannine picked me up at my hotel at 5.30 and we went up to a hotel in Kings Cross to meet with the people I would be working with on the new book. When we arrived, we were standing at the top of the elevator in the hotel and Jane was introducing me to everyone when out of nowhere Mike Munro and a lot of cameras and microphone-booms appeared and Mike said those amazing words, 'Sara Henderson, this is your life!'

Now I was completely at a loss. I was having dinner with my publishers, having a surprise party for my birthday and now was about to go to the television studio for a television show!

Jane calmed me down by saying it was all a set-up and I only had to be at the television show. Everyone had been working behind the scenes for months—they all knew about tonight, except me.

The strange reaction from Marlee when I told her I had booked myself to go to Frankfurt on the 1st October now made sense as the 1st was tonight and I had planned to leave Sydney five hours earlier.

Marlee had called Jane in Sydney and she had called James in Scotland who then called me and told me to delay my trip by one day. Marlee had come up with the family surprise birthday party on the spur of the moment.

I was in a complete daze and for the entire evening I

felt like I was watching the events unfold from the side-line. Which in a way I suppose I was, as my life story was being told as I watched and listened.

Seeing old friends and remembering things that happened so long ago made it a very enjoyable evening and one I will remember forever. After the show finished there was a party which kept going until the people at the studio started pulling the set down around us, preparing for the next day's show. We decided that maybe they wanted us to leave.

The amazing coincidence of the night was the hotel where Mike surprised me. This hotel stands on the same ground as the old Mayfair Hotel once did. The Mayfair was the last hotel my dad managed before he retired and was the very same hotel Charlie lured me to with delightful, but not honourable, intentions. It was the hotel of the exploding bottle of champagne. In *From Strength to Strength* I describe how Charlie took me to Dad's hotel, and ordered dinner in a room he had booked for the night! Not only did the champagne blow its top, Dad also arrived in the room and did the same.

I was given a beautiful Rottie puppy on the show so I named him Munro. He has since grown into a dog the size of a Shetland pony and has the most gentle and delightful manner.

The Frankfurt Book Fair is the experience of a lifetime. Publishers turn up there every year and seem to treat the whole thing as just part of everyday work, but to someone like me it was an out of this world experience.

It took days to see all the publishers' displays, and that

was only the English language section. I did wander into other pavilions but the complex was so vast I thought I could be lost forever. I saw more books in a few days than I have in all my life.

After being home for only one week I left for a five-day book tour of the areas near Sydney we missed on the last tour. We were driving back into the city after the last appointment of the tour when Jane mentioned the launch of Billy Thorpe's book, *Sex and Thugs and Rock 'n' Roll* was being held in the Cross that night. 'Want to go?' She added.

To her amazement I said, 'Yes!'

The launch was in the Mansions Hotel, straight across the street from where the old Mayfair Hotel used to be. So I was back down memory lane again. It was a rowdy night, as you would imagine, but I thoroughly enjoyed myself.

The highlight of the evening was when Jane asked me if I'd like to meet Jack Thompson. He has always reminded me of an Australian version of my Charlie, so of course I said 'Yes!'

Jane introduced us but my name didn't mean anything to him, but he was still very charming. Jane told him a bit more about me and as soon as she mentioned the Outback we had his attention.

He had worked on a cattle station in the Territory when he was young and has loved the place ever since. He talked non-stop as his eyes took on a misty expression. I can tell you one fact about Jack Thompson. Apart from being

211

charming and famous, he truly loves the Northern Territory Outback. Jane took a photo of us while he was talking about the days of his youth. I have included it in this book, because I think the photo says it all. It was a great end to another tour and an end with a difference!

When I arrived home for the wet season, James called and said he had been trying to find me for days. He had in his hand a very important invitation and it had to be answered that day!

'This will be a first for you, I can guarantee that!' he said. I waited.

'It is an invitation from the Prime Minister inviting you to have lunch with the President of the United States! Now what do you think of that!'

It's funny how the mind works, but up to that moment in time I had forgotten about my visit to 1600 Pennsylvania Avenue when Charlie and I had breakfast with President Nixon and his wife back in the late sixties. So I had to say, no, it would be the second time I'd had a meal with a President of the United States.

James's immediate reply was that I had never written about this. I said I was just jotting down a note to do just that in the book I was writing.

My only answer to the 'How could you forget?' question was only, 'I was married to Charlie.' Life with Charlie was like a constant whirlwind. I think I was under so much pressure, just trying to survive that my brain must have divided itself into many separate compartments to cope with the deluge being thrown at it. My brain is now

212

slowly throwing up all these astounding memories.

Well, my lunch with Prime Minister Howard, Mrs Howard, President Clinton and Mrs Clinton was much the same as the breakfast with President Nixon. At least at the breakfast there were only a few hundred people. The lunch had at least twice that number. Politicians crowded around the famous couple for photos and took up all of their time, so the cross-section of Australians who had been invited didn't get to say one word to our American visitors. Despite this, it was a great experience just being there.

There were more conferences and directors' meetings and I made it back home on the 24th November. I had been away so long Munro barked at me with authority and all his hair stood on end. When I spoke to him it triggered something in his memory and the hair went down and the stump of a tail started to wag. Soon his whole body was wagging along with it. He licked me all over in a grand welcome home performance.

Violent storms started early in December as a cyclonic low moved in from the west. We had overcast weather from Christmas Eve to New Year's Day, so we had a wonderful period of cool weather and 1997 arrived quietly amidst soft rain.

CHAPTER 13

January 1997–
February 1997

A phone call from Arthur, Bonnie's estranged
husband, shattered the pleasant start to the new
year. Bonnie was writing a book with a ghostwriter and
by all accounts it was not nice. I put the phone down
after receiving this awful news and felt sick in the pit of
my stomach. Days of turmoil followed with the inevitable question always surfacing. A question I had asked
myself for many years. Why does this daughter of mine
hate me so? I couldn't understand this bitterness. But I
knew this new saga was going to be ongoing and I
would have to get used to it intruding into my life for
the rest of the year.

I was on a very tight schedule to finish my manuscript as I had to hand it in on the 15th March. But
the phone call had put a stop to any creative writing.
I was so upset I didn't put a word on paper for days.
I would sit for hours with pen in hand staring at the

blank page and nothing would happen.

I thought about how much I loved my mother and what a wonderful relationship we had. I compared my childhood and how my mother raised me with Bonnie's childhood and my raising of her, to see if there were any major differences.

When you grow up in an environment where you love your mum and she loves you, I suppose you just automatically think all mothers love their daughters and all daughters return this love. I gave Bonnie all the love I had to give, unconditionally, just as my mum gave to me. I was at a loss when my daughter chose not to love me. This is something I will never come to terms with.

As I sat at my desk these were the thoughts that invaded my mind, denying all other trains of thought. Seeing I was writing a collection of funny stories about the cooks we had had over the years and recipes, this was not a good state to be in! So I struggled for days trying to get through this mental block and slowly and painfully I pushed the hurt away, not to the back of my mind, but out of it all together, and the writing gradually started to flow.

I had settled into a good routine and the pages started to form a neat little pile when I got the second phone call from Arthur with a further update. Suddenly I was back to square one, upset and staring at a blank page again. I could see these awful reports on the contents of this developing book would go on all year.

They not only upset me to the point where I could not write, but filled my life with anguish and stress. Just knowing that this book was going to be eventually

215

printed was enough to make me sick to the stomach, but to receive this ongoing reporting for the whole year was something I knew I could not handle. So after another week or so of complete distress and heartache, I decided I simply would not answer the phone and I turned on the answering machine.

My composure slowly returned, but most of January was gone before I could sit down and think of the job at hand.

January found us still ploughing fields and waiting for rain before we could plant the seed. The hay operation was in full swing, with Marlee and Franz out in the paddocks working around the clock to finish. The work continued right up to the week before Marlee, Franz and Ben were due to depart for Austria so Ben could meet his Austrian family. I wanted so much to pack a bag and disappear to Austria with them but I had to meet the deadline for the manuscript.

I decided to go and stay with Sue and Ralph in Caloundra where I could write undisturbed in peaceful surroundings with no upsetting phone call reaching me.

Marlee knew I was worried about finishing the manuscript on time and she also knew how much distress the latest Bonnie saga was causing me, so to completely remove me from all worry Franz and Marlee handled all the problems of running the station from Austria. The little family were off to Obermillstatt. Marlee's last words to the caretaker were, 'Don't worry Mummy. If you have a problem, call us in Austria!' So I was completely isolated and this was fully enforced by not telling anyone where I was. Alan had my fax number and sent on all the faxes for me received at the station. Luckily the phone calls to Austria were few and between Alan on the station and Geoff Hunt in Darwin, every hitch was solved and Alan called me every few weeks to say all was OK.

Of course our departure had not been without major problems! Our plan was for Franz to fly Marlee and Ben to Darwin so Ben could have his next lot of injections and have a week to recover before the long trip to Europe. Then Franz and I would fly up after the caretaker had settled in and we would have four days together in Darwin before we went our separate ways. Of course the best laid plans are always the ones that come unstuck.

Franz flew Marlee and Ben to Darwin and returned with the caretaker. I left the answering machine on and had a busy writing day. The next day Franz picked up Alan in Kununurra and our caretaking team was in place.

Alan knew the run of the station, but Franz went over the routine with the new man as he was the one who was supposed to do all the work. Alan was just there to answer questions, take care of our dogs and generally keep things on track.

With everyone settled in Franz and I were ready to leave the following morning. We awoke to low menacing clouds stretching as far as the eye could see. A cyclonic low had quietly moved into the valley overnight. Franz got a weather report by fax from the Department of Meteorology and it seemed our track to

Darwin was clear further up the coast. So we took off and headed in a north-easterly direction.

It was soon clear that while the storm was coming from the west, it was also approaching the coast over a vast area from a northerly direction. After ten minutes of flying, the way ahead was not improving and the weather was also moving in behind us. Very soon our only option would be to fly south which would not get us to Darwin or home. The storm was moving so fast that in a short time we would have been flying blind. We headed home posthaste and landed only seconds ahead of an intensive rain squall from the west. By the time we taxied towards the hangar the wind was buffeting the plane. We closed the hangar doors and ran for the house.

So twenty minutes after take-off we were back in the house and drenched to the skin. One look at the sky and weather report told us flying was out for the day. I called Marlee and told her of the delay and said we would see her tomorrow.

The next day there was no improvement in the weather. I called Marlee with the bad news, cancelled the appointments I had for that day, and went on writing.

When the third day dawned with a black sky blocking out the mountains on every side of the valley, we started to worry. By mid-morning the sun broke through the murk, so we decided to try again. The weather seemed to be breaking up and the weather report had it clear around Darwin.

So we set out to find a way through the clouds. We got through the first bank of scattered clouds and sunshine surrounded us. However the way ahead was a different story. We went cold when we saw what we were heading into. A wall of smouldering, twisting, black turbulence was moving towards us. There was no need for conversation. Franz banked sharply and we headed back to the sanctuary of the Bullo valley.

Once more safely on the ground, we now had to admit we had a few problems. The next day at 5 p.m. Marlee and Franz had to check-in at the airport and Marlee was now calling every few hours. At the end of the day it still didn't look good.

We went to bed with glum thoughts of Franz not getting to Darwin in time for the plane to Austria.

The next morning there was a break towards Kununurra. So the next plan—I'd lost count what number we were up to—was to fly to Darwin from Kununurra by jet. The problem was we didn't want to leave our plane parked out in the open at the airport in Kununurra for six weeks in case a cyclone passed through while we were away. So we decided to leave our plane safe and sound on Bullo in the hangar and hire a charter plane.

We unloaded our plane and had the luggage waiting on the airstrip in the Toyota. It only takes thirty-five minutes for a plane to fly from Kununurra to Bullo so after calling Marlee to update her on the latest plan and cancelling more appointments for that day, it was time for the plane to arrive.

We heard the noise of the engine a few minutes later. Franz and I stood out the front of the homestead and watched as the small plane approached. It looked like the plane was not lined up with the airstrip and I

219

commented on this to Franz who said the pilot would probably straighten up closer to touchdown.

He didn't. We watched in amazement as the pilot continued his approach and landed in the ploughed sorghum field right next to the airstrip!

Except for a sharp intake of breath, there was complete silence. After the plane touched down in the field, the nosewheel dug into the soft earth and the propeller hit the ground, spraying up soft dirt. The momentum of the plane had it skidding along on its nose with its tail in the air, ploughing a new row in amongst the new sorghum plants.

The plane then did a very picturesque nosestand for a few seconds with the tail lifting high in the air and balancing on its propeller. We let out a sigh of relief as the plane crashed back down on its wheels rather than flopping on its back. Our eyes searched the scene through the settling dust and we were relieved to see the pilot's door slowly open.

Franz watched through the binoculars and saw the pilot walk away from the plane saying some very choice words by the looks of things. But the important thing was that he appeared not to be injured. Alan drove down the airstrip to bring the pilot back to the house, while Franz called the charter company and in his usual direct manner told them, 'Well, that plane crashed, you had better send us another.' He did go on to elaborate and answered all the questions the worried person at the other end of the phone was asking about the pilot and the state of the plane.

By this time a very pale and shaken pilot had arrived

at the house. We sat him down and handed him the phone so his boss could ask him a few dozen questions. The question we wanted to ask was why, when there was a mowed, one-mile-long grass airstrip with white markers clearly outlining the full length of the strip, would he land in a ploughed field? After the phone call with his boss the pilot asked if he could go back to the plane. So after a cold drink Franz took him back to the crash site and left him sitting forlornly next to the plane. We thought he had a few problems on his mind so we left the obvious question unasked.

By the time two planes landed, one to take us straight back to town, the other bringing in mechanics and various other people from the charter company, to look at the crash site, we were fast running out of time. So we jumped in the plane and took off as everyone on the station headed down to the crash site. We didn't get the answer to our question until much later. It seems the reason he landed where he did was because he had been told that all the airstrips in the North were dirt. So he landed in the ploughed field not on the mowed grass ten feet away. We were not surprised when we heard the pilot had gone back down south.

While the pilot was on the ground at Bullo trying to explain why he missed a marked airstrip by ten feet, we had our own problems in the air. We were racing to catch the jet to Darwin and ten minutes out from Kununurra we knew we were going to miss it. Our pilot called his base and told them to ask Ansett to hold the jet for a few minutes as we were on our way. Luckily they said 'Yes'!

We landed and taxied over to the steps of the jet, where two of the Ansett staff were waiting. They put luggage tags on our suitcases and whisked them away and handed us boarding passes. We dashed up the stairs and sagged into our seats and the door slammed shut behind us.

We arrived in Darwin at 3 p.m., with just a few hours to spare before departure time. Marlee and Ben met us at the airport, very pleased to see us indeed. Ben put his arms out and had such an expression of joy on his face, we were in no doubt at all that he had missed his papa and nana.

I had a quiet day the day after their departure, spending it in the beauty salon. I had been out on the station for months and needed a major body overhaul to get every-thing back into 'town' condition. I stepped on the plane to Brisbane the next day a new woman.

Only hours after settling into the tranquil atmosphere of my sister's home I received a phone call from Marlee. Everyone loved Ben, of course, and they were staying in Franz's auntie's summer house right down on the lake. Mama Ranacher had thought of everything includ-ing the food and even winter clothes for little Ben, so Marlee had walked into a fully stocked and running house. I wished them a wonderful holiday and settled in for six weeks of intensive writing.

I started writing at 4 a.m. each morning and apart from a lunch break and a swim, I worked through to six and sometimes seven o'clock each night. I did take

Sundays off and with Ralph, Susan, Tod and Frances went to some lovely restaurants in the area.

About midway through this manic writing schedule, on Valentine's Day, Martin called from Mount Isa to say Danielle had just had a little baby boy.

I finished the manuscript the day before I was due to fly home. So I had one day off! I spent this rare day sitting on the verandah staring out to sea wondering what life would be like with nothing to do. Although it's something I don't think I will ever experience.

I flew home the next day. Marlee and Franz were already home and they looked rested and well despite a week of heavy work getting the station ready to start the season. Ben had grown so much in the six weeks. He wasn't too sure who I was for a few days, but I gave him his space. On the third day, when Marlee was standing talking to me and holding him in her arms, he put out his little arms to me.

I sat him on my lap as I always did as I watched the news. He sat quietly holding my hand and we watched the news together.

223

CHAPTER 14

March 1997–
September 1997

It was a busy beginning to the mustering season. Marlee's first job was to open the road and Franz had his hands more than full with baling hay.

Then we worked to get the house back in running order. We had to reclaim the lawn which was now two-feet tall and repairs were needed everywhere. It seemed that no matter which direction you looked, something required attention. Marlee and Franz had been working for over a week when I arrived home and the homestead and garden were only just starting to show improvement.

If you stood still for a moment you could hear the place humming with activity. Inside, months of cobwebs and dust were being swept away, and outside machine engines were revving, along with all the noises of cranking up the station for a new season.

Most of our staff for the season had settled in and were

working. And the building of the new staff sleeping quarters was well on its way which was fortunate because most of the stockmen were camping out under the stars waiting until they could occupy the new rooms.

The demolition of the rest of the old bedrooms was done fairly quickly. After many years of being infested with white ants, the building had had many braces, supports and patches applied in our vain attempt to keep it standing. Add to that a few very violent storms during the last rainy season and you had a very flexible building. It was only necessary to remove a few strategic supports and it basically sagged gracefully to the ground. One of the stockmen watching said that every time he had turned over in bed last season the wall moved!

So the staff were spread out over a wide selection of jobs when our first visitors of the year arrived—the Breast Screen crew ready to take a new series of photos for magazines and to record some more radio ads.

It was a meeting of old friends. As this was their second time on Bullo there was no need for the usual few days for visitors to settle into the Outback routine. Marlee and I had been in contact with Shirley Howlett from the advertising agency many times since the last visit and she knew it was Marlee's birthday the day after their arrival. So for a birthday surprise, Shirley brought a magnificent chocolate mud cake for Marlee and we had a birthday party the first night which set a terrific mood for the whole shoot.

Over the next four days I smiled at the camera for

hours on end. Ben joined me and became quite the little performer. He smiled on cue virtually every time the camera came his way. Being the second shoot, it was an easy and enjoyable process. This time I knew what to expect and the crew knew the ins and outs of living in the Outback. They knew not to drink the bore water, knew where they could find the cold rainwater tap and knew not to leave lights on in their room or they would have a few thousand bugs sharing their bed for the night. The best thing about the shoot was that we were working in April so although it was still hot, it was much cooler than the January shoot.

The days passed quickly and productively. I knew this by the aching smile muscles in my face! At every opportunity I did my face-relaxing exercises. So if I wasn't smiling at the camera I looked like a comedian trying to imitate a blowfish!

The last day of the visit was Ben's birthday. The cake, also brought from Melbourne, was bright blue and in the shape of a number one. There was a fantastic photo taken of Ben sitting on my knee, looking at his first birthday cake with complete wonderment.

We waved goodbye as the crew's plane disappeared into the cloudy sky and ambled back to the cool of the homestead. But there was no time for feet up for us. Apart from the full-on station program, we were soon onto the next big project. In only a matter of days we had another team in for a photo shoot. This time would require a lot more input from us.

The shoot was for the food layouts for my new book. And here we were with our dear old electric stove still standing and only working when it felt like it. I was having nightmares about trying to explain to two food stylists, no less, the mathematical equations necessary just to set the oven on the required temperature. This was the result of Uncle Dick 'repairing' the heat thermostat. It never worked again. The nightmares got worse with scenes of the oven just refusing to work or stopping in the middle of baking a cake.

The thought of two chefs in the kitchen trying to cook in Uncle Dick's oven got too much for me, so it was off to Darwin to buy a new oven.

We still had to cook meals for the staff and crew and I couldn't see two teams of cooks working in the one kitchen—even in one as big as ours—and producing on schedule. So I set up a second kitchen for the chefs around the new stove, in the area between the kitchen-sink area and the dining room. It didn't look much, and certainly wouldn't have won any Kitchen of the Year awards, but it was functional. I apologised to the food stylists for their makeshift kitchen but they were delighted with it, telling me they mostly cooked in cramped corners.

Meanwhile, back in the old kitchen we struggled on with the dear old electric oven which continued to stop working at regular intervals.

This shoot had many problems, not the least being when it was discovered a part of the camera needed to shoot the cover photograph of the book was left in Sydney. I handed this problem over to Marlee and no-one could believe it, but we had the part in our hot little hands the

227

next morning at 9 a.m. This was a miracle—ask anyone who's tried to get freight to Darwin from down south.

After solving this problem, the others that presented themselves seemed minor. It was a successful shoot with some great photos of Bullo as the background to some stunning food shots. Even the snakes stayed away from the house and didn't scare the living daylights out of any of our city guests.

With these two big projects out of the way we were able to pay full attention to station work. Work was going on all through the photo shoots, but there were continual delays such as when I was being photographed in the sorghum field and the mower and the baler had to stop to wait for the shots to be completed. People also needed to be taken to different locations so stock-men became guides and drivers.

By the first week of May baling was well and truly on its way and the new bedrooms were almost finished. This was another giant step in the development of the station. The staff were lining up, ready to take possession as soon as the floor tiles were put down, but we had to delay them a few more days while the cement verandah around the rooms was laid. By the end of the week everyone had finally moved in and they were very pleased with the new accommodation.

A vast improvement on what was pulled down, the new building boasted flyscreen doors, fans, sliding glass doors and properly wired lighting. The old rooms had wires hanging out of the walls where staff had ripped out and taken wall mounted reading lamps with them when they left!

The new quarters looked slightly out of place—modern and sparkling new—standing next to the old rusty red tin shed which still housed the bathrooms, toilets, kitchen and dining area. It was next on the replacement agenda, but had to stay put for the moment, propped up with many supports. It would be on next year's schedule, maybe . . .

The hay was baled, stacked and fenced in by mid-May. Then we were ready to start our first horse muster in the close paddocks before bringing in the cattle from further afield with the helicopters.

We had very late, quite heavy rain and the weather remained unsettled. A few days later I received a phone call from the police at Timber Creek. They called to inform us that a Qantas pilot flying over the Indian Ocean heading for the north-west coast of Australia had spotted a tidal wave about 120 miles offshore. It looked large from 42,000 feet and it was heading in a direction that would have it hitting the tip of the north-west corner of Western Australia. The police had no idea when the tidal wave was expected to hit the coast, how high it was, or how fast it was travelling. But they said we should take precautions for massive tides—seeing we are on the Victoria River and close to the sea we were sure to be affected. What precautions one takes for a tidal wave I was not exactly sure, but the word 'high ground' kept coming to mind!

March 1997–September 1997

As is always the case, I was home alone and no-one would be back till mid-afternoon. They were out of reach of the two-way radio and just happened to be building yards down near the Victoria River. I waited by the phone for more news. There was a rough estimate given that the tidal wave would take around twelve hours to reach the Joseph Bonaparte Gulf then had forty miles to travel up the Victoria to reach us.

So I was sure we wouldn't have a hundred-foot wall of water descending upon us, but I was still worried.

I decided if I didn't receive some news in the next few hours, I would drive down to Bull Creek and tell Marlee and Franz we had a tidal wave on the way. After a few more hours of worry and no news I called Darwin. I was relieved to hear the tidal wave had fizzled out and had simply disappeared.

The following day we had to put our darling Bootsie down. What a terrible day that was! He had hurt his shoulder, doing what came naturally, namely being a stallion. Sarah had come out to the station to look at him a few weeks earlier, when he first had the accident. She thought the shoulder might only be cracked because he could still walk fairly well. So we persevered and tried to bring him through his latest injury.

He was a good patient and he had the company of his favourite mare, Goldie, who was also in sickbay with a bad cut. They spent their days in the covered horse yard, eating and lapping up all the attention. Boots limped around for weeks and seemed to be progressing well. Marlee gave him painkillers while the healing process was going on and he seemed quite happy. He was eating well and that was usually a good indicator of Boots's health as he loved his food. But after weeks of TLC he lost interest in his food. We tried everything we could to get him to eat, but sadly had to admit there was nothing more that could be done.

I couldn't bear to say goodbye, it was just too much to handle and even Marlee chickened out on this one. Franz, bless his heart, laid our darling Boots to rest under the old bottle tree with our other loved pets.

After a few days of tears I wandered over and had a chat with him, thanking him for being such a wonderful part of my life, and telling him I would never forget him.

A few days later I saw the silhouette of Marlee's hat against the setting sun as she made her way through the paddock to Bootsie's resting place. She didn't get back to the homestead for quite a while as she had a lot to say to her old friend.

Early the next morning as I walked out onto the lawn after a brief heavy shower of rain I saw two rainbows stretching right across the valley. It was such a beautiful sight it cheered me a little and I thought maybe Bootsie was saying hello in his usual notable way from his new home.

It was just going to be one of those years. I could feel it in my bones. 'Well,' I told myself, 'You have had a lot of practice at living through problem years.' So I decided to get on with it and get the year over as fast as I possibly could.

231

Apart from our new staff quarters, the biggest event this year on Bullo had to be the new roof on the homestead.

The roof on the homestead was on a par with, if not in worse condition than, the old staff quarters. Each year, for longer than I care to remember, I have been waiting for the roof to either blow away in a violent storm or simply fall down on top of us. Ten years ago Uncle Dick welded two large steel frames under the ceiling in the living room after he had been up into the ceiling to repair an electrical cable. What he saw had convinced him if he didn't put supports under the ceiling, it would soon be on the floor.

These temporary supports were still there and doing a good job of keeping the ceiling in place. But one year during a very turbulent storm, a twister came whooshing through the living room and the entire ceiling lifted up in the air. I watched it float high in the air, a few feet clear of the supporting beams, and waited for it to come crashing down on the floor. Instead, it just settled gracefully back into place on the supports. Builders years ago certainly knew how to put a building together. The ceiling may have sagged eighteen inches, but it has stayed in one piece.

I can't say the same for the additions that were added to the old tin shed over the years. Every join in it leaked and it was still raining inside the house ten minutes after it had stopped outside. Every year we rearranged the furniture to avoid the leaks.

I was so looking forward to a roof that didn't leak, but I knew this was not going to be an easy project. First to go were all my trees growing up through the roof. I lost a lime tree, a bottle tree that was taking over one of the guest rooms and my very favourite coconut tree that went up through the roof in the living room.

This was the most difficult tree to remove because it was extremely tall. It was the first tree I planted when I came to Bullo. Being a complete gardening beginner, I planted four coconut trees around the children's swimming pool for shade! I had no idea at the time how long these trees needed to grow and that they still would not provide shade over the pool twenty years later.

During the expansion of the homestead this tree became part of the living room. It was quite a topic of conversation as people were fascinated to see a tree growing up through the roof in the middle of a room.

How to get the tree down was the big problem. If we just cut it and let it fall it would crash into the walls of the living room. But Franz worked out a system. The tree was to be cut down in three sections. Because of its height, there was too much danger in being up a ladder cutting with a chain saw when the first section fell. So Franz cut halfway through the trunk with the chainsaw, then climbed down and he shot through the rest of the trunk with a high-powered rifle. The bullets cut through the soft trunk and the top of the tree toppled after only a few shots. Of course it does help to be a good shot to achieve this desired effect! The top of the tree gracefully fell and was stopped from crashing into the old roof and walls by rope and tackle.

The next fifteen feet went the same way. But being solid trunk this was heavier and the guide ropes slipped slightly letting the end of the tree crash into the roof with a resounding thud. It cut a massive slash through the tin roof, giving us a fair indication of what the whole tree would have done to the roof and walls.

The third part of the tree was cut in two sections, about five feet to the roof level and the rest of the ten feet inside the living room.

We still have a three-foot stump in the house. I can't imagine how much floor would have to be dug up to get the root system out! So for the time being I have put a large reclining stone giraffe on the stump and surrounded it with ferns so it gives the pleasant appearance of the animal sitting in a garden.

When at long last I could finally see work starting and this new roof becoming a reality, I was very keen to get things moving. How different my thoughts were in the following months when tonnes of dust showered into rooms as the men went about their demolition with gusto.

Phone calls were next to impossible, so I timed my calls between drilling, electric saws and jemmies reefing tin from the roof. Life somehow continued amidst the mayhem as Franz and his merry team pulled the roof apart above our heads. I found it was very wise to look up before venturing into any part of the house!

Marlee finished the road and not a moment too soon as we were out of cooking gas. The electric oven was up to its usual tricks, only working when it felt like it and amidst all this confusion, the new cook arrived.

We had planned to go to town the week before

because we knew our gas supply was low, but Kununurra was out of cooking gas, so we waited for the new supply to arrive from Perth before we left for town, and we ran out the day before. Marlee left me with the new cook, Ben and Lita, Ben's nanny, and was off to town for a fresh food order and cooking gas. The electric oven went on strike again, so I told the cook to make meals that could be cooked on the electric cooktop until Marlee returned with the gas.

I had my head in my writing and lost track of time. I realised by late afternoon that Marlee had not called to say what time she was leaving town.

I called the supermarket to see what time Marlee picked up the order, so I would know when to expect her, and my heart hit the floor when the girl said the order was still there! Two quick calls to the Kununurra and Timber Creek police made my heartbeat slow down slightly. They assured me there had been no accidents on the Victoria Highway that day. If she had broken down on the highway I would have heard from her. So the only place she could be was on our road . . . again.

When Franz walked in the door at 6 p.m. I had an esky ready filled with sandwiches, fruit, water and drinks and he dashed straight out the door. I had dinner and watched a movie to pass the time.

When Franz and Marlee hadn't arrived home by 10.30—time enough for him to drive to the front gate and back—I sent out the back-up rescue team. Paul, our NZ stockman, and Lita set off in the other Toyota.

By now I was too worried to watch a movie so I took a chair out on the lawn and just stared down the road, waiting to see the first flicker of headlights through the trees about three miles away. Jennifer, our new cook, joined me and there we sat in silent vigil.

At 11.15 a great wave of relief washed over me when I saw headlights way off through the trees. We started chatting immediately. The vehicle had to go through three gates in the last three miles so it was a lengthy wait for their arrival.

The second Toyota had been making a funny clunking noise so Paul thought it best to come back before it broke down. The plan now was to drive out in one of the stockmen's utilities which was new and much more reliable.

Jennifer and I sat back down with a hot cup of tea and the dogs gathered around. The cold night settled around us and we sat in silence, eyes glued to the road. Frightening images flashed into my brain and my only movements over the next hour were regular trips to Ben's room to see if he was still asleep.

Lights! Our chatter started almost immediately and the dogs jumped around feeling the change of mood.

People streamed in every door, all talking at once and Marlee and Franz settled down to a midnight dinner. We all sat in the kitchen to hear the different sagas. At 8.00 a.m. Marlee had heard a whine from the gearbox about thirty-five miles down the road. On stopping the car she discovered the plug had come out of the bottom of the gearbox and there was no oil. She had the choice of either sitting and waiting or walking back to the homestead. Marlee knew we would be along eventually so she decided to wait.

236

In case Franz came looking for her in the plane, she wrote a message on the road with toilet paper and rope: 'Gear oil, no plug'. She passed the day cleaning the station wagon, and with a few walks and a few naps. She also made a note to herself to keep a supply of reading matter in the car.

At ten o'clock she saw torchlight and along came Franz. Walking! A mile back down the road he'd had a flat tyre and someone had taken the wheel spanner out of the Toyota's toolkit and not put it back. Franz knew Marlee was somewhere in the next fifteen miles of the road so he started walking to find her and get the wheel spanner out of her toolkit.

Together they walked back to the Toyota and changed the flat tyre. They then drove back to Marlee's vehicle and picked up that spare in case they had another flat on the drive home. They met the rescue team eighteen miles from the homestead.

We all went to bed around 1 a.m., still out of cooking gas and lots of food. There would be no eggs and bacon for Sunday breakfast, but I didn't mind, my prayers had been answered and everyone was delivered home safely. I went to bed thinking, 'Just another day in the Outback.'

One piece of good news came my way in April: my first book was published in Holland. I received some copies and it was a strange feeling to look at my book in a foreign language. The Dutch title was *Met Blote Handen*, which roughly translated means *With Bare*

Hands. A friend who lives in Holland called and said the translation was excellent. She had read my book in English and so was in a good position to judge.

This news came as we were sending our first lot of sale cattle to market, so I hoped that the bad start to the year had run its course. Good things kept coming and in one day I received calls from book readers in Tasmania, Queensland, New South Wales, Wiltshire, England and Long Island, New York.

We sent another load of steers to Darwin before the gloom settled over not only our lives, but over the lives of all the cattle people of the North.

Overnight the markets to South East Asia disappeared. When Marlee called to sell our next load of cattle in July the exporter said our main markets—Indonesia and the Philippines—had temporarily suspended all purchase of cattle. Our questions of 'Why?' and 'For how long?' received no satisfactory answers. No-one seemed to know why.

We had sent off only half of our usual cattle for the season, so we decided to turn to culling our herd and selling to the local abattoir. We put a decent line of fairly well-covered cattle into the yards and when the abattoir buyer arrived we were speechless when he offered us ten dollars a head for two hundred. We would usually receive about $150 per head.

Marlee controlled her temper and smiled at him sweetly, but burst into my office wanting to 'do him in'! She asked me what I thought and I said I would rather let them live out their life on Bullo and go to sleep under a tree of old age than sell them for that price.

So she politely told him, 'No sale'!

After this shocking offer from the only abattoir in the district we had nowhere else to sell our cattle, so decided to cut back on staff and wait till the next season. The experts said everything would be back to normal by the end of the year, so we decided to pull in our belts for the rest of the season and wait till then.

Mustering was put on hold and we concentrated on the homestead roof. There was a bit of urgency for this project as we had a group of thirty people arriving a few weeks later. They were interested in Bazadaise cattle and Bernie O'Kane had organised for them to come and spend four days on Bullo. When I reminded Marlee we had no roof she assured me it was all right. These people, she told me, were self-sufficient and wouldn't be bothering us at all and would probably camp at six-mile. From experience I knew this to be completely wrong so my aim in the following weeks was to get the roof finished and the furniture back in the house, ready to receive the guests!

What a few weeks it was. As the old roof was pulled off and thrown on the ground, memories came flooding back of the building of that roof. I couldn't help but notice the speed and ease of building the new roof compared with building the original back in the seventies. Then it was done with 44-gallon drums balanced on the trays of Toyotas, lots of manpower and much swearing.

239

Now I stood and watched the new roof go on with Marlee driving the frontend loader and Franz driving the backhoe/loader, lifting forty-foot steel beams into place with no fuss and then held there as the welding was done. What a difference a few machines make!

I'm sure by now you have guessed that the roof was still being finished as the guests were driving down the last mile of our road. It wasn't so much the roof that was bothering me but the mess inside! We had all been sweeping for days and when the staff left I would continue well into the night. But dust seemed to come from everywhere and after sweeping and vacuuming more dust would appear.

As the convoy of vehicles drove into the garden we were still dusting, sweeping and putting furniture back into the living room. Marlee's famous words of them being self-sufficient and camping up at six-mile came back to haunt her. They camped in the garden and the first thing they did when they arrived was head for the homestead, straight into the pandemonium of the living room.

That night when we were alone in the living room still dusting and arranging furniture, Marlee said, 'Don't say, "I told you so"!'

As the cattle crisis worsened, Marlee, Franz and I all felt this was going to be a long-term thing. Not a few months, or even a season, of no sales as the experts believed. So I thought this would be a good time to diversify again. Australian Pacific Tours had been asking

240

us to consider having bus tours come to Bullo for a few years. We had been putting this off, mainly because of the nightmares I had of buses getting bogged along our road, but with doubts of any cattle sales for the next year or more, we now had to look at this income opportunity more seriously. I called Dino Magris from the tour group and we discussed a few ideas. We ended up agreeing to give their clients the option of flying into Bullo once they arrived in Kununurra. We were committed to buses passing through our area from November 1998 on an average of twice a week. The people are on an around Australia holiday and when they reach Kununurra they have a few options. Coming to Bullo for afternoon tea became one of the options for 1998. We were back in the tourist business, and I hoped it would be in a big way as cattle were not looking like a good bet.

This venture proved to be a very fortunate move because a few months later the Asian economic meltdown happened. I couldn't help but wonder after getting over the shock of no cattle market for the next few years, why, when most of the countries stopped buying cattle back in July, didn't the economic experts see the meltdown coming?

We hoped our switch to tourism would help us through what was predicted to be at least a two-year slump.

The year was continuing on its miserable way and I still had a fair way to go!

Board meetings, the Order of Australia Council and conferences kept me travelling. When I did make it home, I would catch up on the office work as it was time to send in the figures for the end of the financial year.

There was just no time at all to read the mail from all my readers, so it just kept piling up in one corner of the room. But my readers have caught on and now send me faxes, so the fax machine ground along all day.

My readers know I read the faxes within weeks or months of receiving them, as against the letters which sometimes don't get read for years.

I received a lovely fax from Mandy, saying,

After reading your work I felt that your daughter had a lovely personality and a strength of character that I always wished for in my children. Hence I chose to name my darling after your daughter.

Yes, she named her daughter Marlee!

In late August I was off travelling again and only days before I was scheduled to leave, I had a visit from a very old friend indeed. Bob Goddard is the American Charles and I met in the Kununurra Hotel way back in 1970. Bob had heard Charlie talking, which was not hard if you were within a city block of him, and being another (but quietly spoken) American a long way from home, he came over to our table and introduced himself. By the time Charlie had finished talking, Bob was under

242

the impression that Charlie owned half of Australia. Bob being a quiet and modest man didn't even get the chance to present his credentials, which were in oil in Texas and very impressive and, unlike Charlie's, were true.

I will never forget the look on Bob's face when he arrived at Bullo and walked into our tin shed. Charles led the way as if he was walking into the White House.

So Bob, with his wife Dorothy, was back at Bullo after twenty-seven years. It probably took that long to get over Charlie and the tin shed. This visit he was very complimentary about how we had turned the station around. He had followed the Henderson saga since his first visit and told me he didn't think the place could be saved after Charlie died and left us in so much debt.

A thank you letter from himself and Dorothy after they arrived home said that Bullo was the highlight of their trip. This was something he hadn't expressed after his 1970 visit!

The next day I flew to Darwin for R & M (repair and maintenance). Because, apart from a few conferences and the Order of Australia Council meeting and a meeting with my publisher, James, I had been invited to dinner with the Governor General and Lady Deane. Along with the rest of the members of the Order of Australia Council, of course. After a day in the beauty salon and at the hairdresser I was off to the big smoke.

Dinner at Government House was just wonderful. Australia's traditions and past are evident in every inch

243

of Government House and I felt extremely proud to be an Australian.

I was seated next to the Governor General and was very nervous the entire time, ready to knock over my wineglass or something. But Sir William Deane is a charming host and puts people at their ease. Before I knew it I was telling him a joke about cattle that he could use in his next speech to cattle people a few weeks later!

I was home for my birthday which was very unusual, but wonderful. Family called to wish me happy sixtieth birthday, and my sister Sue told me it was all downhill from now on! A surprising number of readers remembered and called me or sent faxes. Marlee cooked me a wonderful birthday dinner with all the food no-noes I only have on Mother's Day and my birthday. Ben gave me a kiss but was more interested in getting closer to the birthday cake!

CHAPTER 15

October 1997–
December 1997

October was soon upon me and it was time to leave for my book tour for *A Year at Bullo*. This was a big tour—twenty-six jam-packed days.

The Bonnie saga had been raising its ugly head all year and now I was starting my tour it was back in full force with nasty articles in newspapers.

Her book was finally published and it was not a nice book—not about me, anyway. The whole exercise was about riding on the coattails of my books.

So it was with a heavy heart that I started my book tour. So many emotions had to be conquered during the months leading up to the tour and during the tour itself. It would take a whole book to explain the feelings of a mother who finally had to admit to herself that her daughter hates her.

A normal tour is draining enough, but to have to fight for control of your emotions every second for twenty-six days was a first for me. A strange mix of emotions coursed through my body and October was one of the most difficult, nightmarish and heartbreaking, yet rewarding, times of my life.

It appeared that everything was being done to link this book as closely with me as possible. Nasty articles came out in each city, staged to appear when I was there. I was told that they even tried to book Bonnie into every town I was speaking in, but a few days behind me.

But an amazing thing happened. The people made their presence felt in support of me and there were such dismal bookings in most places that her tour gradually petered out.

This didn't ease the pressure on me, however, as people had read the outrageous articles in the papers and were naturally curious. So I was asked questions about this by newspaper journalists and television and radio hosts and I dreaded each day.

I had no idea how to handle a daughter who didn't love me and chose to put it in print. Where do you start?

I had no answer to any of the questions that flooded my head day and night. My entire being was in turmoil during the first few days of the tour and I knew I couldn't continue like this for twenty-six days.

So I took the best course of action I knew. I chose to ignore the whole sordid affair and concentrate wholly on my tour. I had not read her book at this stage and was determined not to do so until after my tour.

About four days into the tour the questions about Bonnie from the media decreased. Only a few questions came from the audience the whole tour and I answered these by saying how I felt as a mother, and what heartbreak it had caused. People were very kind and after the first week even the media stopped asking questions.

I started hearing amazing stories of people abusing bookstore owners for stocking Bonnie's book. Other people said they would never buy another book from a store if they stocked her dreadful book.

After the first few days, my emotions settled and I stopped feeling like I was under attack. I realised I had been waiting for hostile questions and reasoned that this attitude would only invite further questions of this type. So I relaxed, smiled and waited and everything changed.

I could feel the strength from the people. I could physically feel their goodwill and support washing over me when I spoke at functions. Sometimes I could read the expression in a woman's eye which would tell me, 'I know what you are going through, I am going through the same thing.'

Some women just held my hand and looked into my eyes and I knew they had lived through the same turmoil.

This book tour turned into an amazing journey through human emotions. So many feelings and thoughts passed between people, and although nothing was said, emotions were clearly understood. As distressed as I was, I would not have missed the experience for anything. The silent support given to me every place I visited on the tour will be etched in my heart forever.

At the end of the last day of the tour, in Perth, I had to admit I was utterly exhausted. I had two days to myself before I was to speak at Murdoch University to raise funds for the world-class work done by their Department of Veterinary Sciences.

As I sat in my hotel room, completely drained, I knew that sitting in my suitcase in a brown paperbag was the reason for all my emotional trauma.

Earlier in the tour I had been given Bonnie's book and true to my promise had not opened it. I had found the newspaper articles at the time so upsetting that it took me days to bring my emotions back under control, so I knew I could not read it at the same time as I was touring.

I sat and stared at the suitcase for a long time. Did I need to read this book? Why not just forget its existence? I should have filed it away as a bad experience that was in the past. I should have ... but I didn't.

The mother part of me had to read the book, so I walked over to the suitcase, slipped the book out of its hiding place, and settled down on the bed and turned to the first page.

The sun was low in the sky and a tray of lunch remained untouched at the foot of the bed when I closed the back cover. I stared out the window at the setting sun and the sailing boats which moved across the wide expanse of water that filled my view. I didn't notice the tears until they had filled my eyes and blurred my vision.

A strange feeling gripped me. Other than the tears blurring the view, there was no sobbing, no flood of tears streaming down my face, no raging emotions, no anger, no aching heart.

My reaction to what I had just read surprised me. 'Do

I feel anything?' I asked myself. 'Yes,' came the answer. I did feel one emotion. I felt all-encompassing pity for this daughter of mine. Pity because she had denied herself a mother's love, pity because it was clear to me that she was a sad person, and pity because I had to finally admit to myself that she hated me. I pitied this lost soul with all my heart.

I blinked away the tears and the view jumped back into sharp focus. I watched the boats moving across the water and thought of Charlie. After a long period of thought, I put the book down and knew with that simple action I had also laid to rest, once and for all, the major heartbreak of my life.

The next day I rested, had a massage and found a hairdresser to do something with my hair. I shared a great evening with the Murdoch University's Department of Veterinary Sciences and the people who supported their endeavours. The dinner was very successful and the big surprise of the night was seeing Jacqui, our one and only wonderful housekeeper who was there with Ethnée Holmes à Court. I originally met Ethnée through Jacqui, who before working on Bullo was in charge of the mares and foaling at Heytesbury Stud. Ethnée had visited Jacqui at Bullo a few years ago. She called me a year ago and said she was interested in writing her life story. I put her in touch with James and the result was a book deal—her book will be launched just a few weeks after I finish this manuscript.

I flew home the next day. This tour would certainly stand out as different from all others. But apart from the terrible Bonnie saga, there were some events on this tour that would stay with me forever for much nicer reasons.

On day one I was interviewed by John Laws. You would think that by now, after seven years of being interviewed, I would be comfortable with the routine. No such luck. I was so nervous before this interview I was on the verge of breaking out in hives. A mouthful of tea just stopped midthroat and wouldn't go down! I panicked. I couldn't speak and just hoped I wouldn't choke. Seeing it wouldn't go down, I thought I had better get it back up. Everyone was talking so I turned my back and just spat the mouthful of tea back into the cup. I put the cup back on the table with a shaky hand.

Then the terrible thought hit me, that maybe I couldn't speak! I joined the conversation with a rush, my voice was squeaky and high, but it settled down after the first few words.

After averting this minor disaster I just reverted to being terrified about the impending interview. The red light turned to green over the door and it was all systems go and I felt like a lamb being led to the slaughter. I really couldn't remember when I had been so nervous.

Luckily, it was all wasted emotion. He is the most charming man and put me at ease within seconds. It was a very long interview and the nerves were still there, but just under the surface. I left the studio after an hour and was just as nervous when I walked out the door as I had been when I walked in.

I am sure the heightened state of my nerves was due

250

to the Bonnie saga. On top of this, being interviewed by the 'great one' of radio first up was a bit much for my nervous system.

The next highlight of the tour was my interview with Kerri-Anne on *Midday*. By this time, excerpts from Bonnie's book had been in the weekend press and I knew there would be questions as she had basically contradicted just about everything I said in my books.

I think Kerri-Anne sensed my emotional state and it was a very caring interview.

Kerri-Anne had been the first person to interview me after I won the Businesswoman of the Year Award, on *Good Morning Australia*. It was the first time I had ever been on television and I was terrified. Here I was seven years later, still terrified, but for much more heartbreaking reasons.

During the tour I found myself signing books in the most peculiar places. My dentist gave me an injection for a filling and left the room while the drug was taking effect. One of his staff ducked in the door and asked me to sign a book for her mother. This was the easy task. Trying to answer questions with a bottom lip rapidly going numb and feeling the size of a football was the hard part!

Still with half my face numb I was going up in the lift in the hotel after my dental appointment and a woman said, 'Excuse me but are you Sara Henderson?

251

Isn't this amazing, I just bought your book!'

Luckily she didn't require spoken answers and I did a lot of nodding and smiling.

'Would you sign it for me?'

More nodding!

I went to her floor and waited by the lift. She rushed back with the book which I signed. I managed to get out a few words and I think she understood I had just been to the dentist!

The next day in the beauty salon, on the waxing table, a head came around the corner of the curtain. This woman had recognised me when we passed each other at the door and had rushed downstairs to buy my book in the newsagency. The book was thrust at me and as I sat wrapped in a towel, carefully trying not to get wax on everything or glue my legs together, I signed the book for one happy woman.

In the jet flying from Darwin to Sydney, the air hostess was reading my book and just happened to have it with her. So I signed that one too.

During this time Marlee was busy trucking some sale cattle to market. We had been lucky to get an overseas sale, as well as some sales to a small abattoir close by in Kununurra. This was welcome news and a great boost to the budget at this time of the year.

I arrived home to a request to have a racehorse named after me! I was quite honoured but I hoped it wasn't going to run at my present speed. Although back in the old days I was a bit of a sprinter at school.

This young horse had a lot of top racing blood in her veins and I was thrilled that someone wanted to name her after me.

Unfortunately some of my contractual obligations made it impossible for me to allow a racehorse to be running around a race track with my name.

The year was drawing to a close and I was anxious for this particular one to finish. But November did have some highlights. It was Natalie's birthday on the 9th and we had the first storm of the season the day before. And what a storm it was. Hailstones the size of golfballs were being blown in the arches of the homestead and skated across the living room floor. I looked up at our new roof and sighed. What a blessing. If the old roof had been still in place it would not have stayed around for long!

Animals were running around in panic not knowing what was hurting their backs as the hailstones struck them. We had 20 millimetres in fifteen minutes. And our fingers were crossed for lots more of the rain, but less of the violence.

I was off south again for the last time that year. I went to my last director's meeting for the year and had a meeting with a producer and director about a four-hour miniseries of *From Strength to Strength*. I walked away from this meeting knowing that this was not going to be easy, but I liked the people so that was the first hurdle.

I arrived home before the end of the month and it

253

was straight into writing. The pressure was now on as I was fast running out of time. I really didn't have my teeth into this book yet, just lots of stories and the five-year record in diary form.

The storms were coming thick and fast. If this kept up we would have a record wet. And didn't we need it! Windchimes heralded the next storm, along with Barpee, our cockatiel. Marlee bought the little bird for Ben and when she asked Ben what name did he think we should give the little bird he came out with something that sounded like 'Barpee'. The chimes were clanging unmelodiously and Barpee's shrill calls for rescue had us all running. The winds, only a week before, had been so strong the poor little bird was plastered up against the side of his cage, unable to move, only squark. He was very relieved when we moved his cage out of the wind tunnel. But remembering this first experience, he was instantly alerted by the wild melodies of the windchimes and started squarking to be rescued.

By the end of November all the staff had departed, with yet another couple in love! This is now one couple struck by cupid's arrow each year for six years. At present there have been three marriages with two of them going well with three children and the other one finished. There has also been one engagement with the wedding happening soon.

The house was very quiet after everyone departed, but after such a turbulent year just to be with family for the first time in many months was great.

It was soon December which meant full-time writing for me. The weather was quickly changing with the monsoonal trough slowly settling over the North giving the comforting feeling of good rains to come.

Storms were almost daily now and the valley was turning a deep, rich green. I watched the storms cause havoc as they swept into the valley with winds so strong even the geese had trouble pitching on the front lawn. They hovered above the ground, flying into the wind, struggling not to be swept away. They then waited for the lulls in between the gusts so they could swoop down and land gracefully. There were some whose timing was a bit off, the landings reminiscent of our brolga Bleep learning to fly.

After I finished my writing one day I watched the movement of the trees and crops in the fields intensify as wind swept into the valley. My eyes lifted to the horizon and I saw the next storm moving swiftly towards the valley. It was a massive front, reaching from mountain range to mountain range and towering tens of thousands of feet into the air. In its wake was rolling turbulence sucking in dust and grass as it steamrolled across the valley.

The Outback never ceases to amaze me. It always manages to produce something new. I had been alerted to this storm by the screeching of hundreds of cockatoos. An entire flock was caught in the raging vortex before the storm. Helpless in its grip, they protested loudly as they were swept along in the whirlwind. In

255

short lulls, as the raging wind took a deep breath, birds fell out of the whirlpool and found themselves left behind on the ground as the storm continued on its way with the rest of their flock.

I watched the lightning bounce off the mountains and the colours of the valley deepen as the sun disappeared behind blue-black clouds.

The few hundred geese had taken up residence in Marlee's birdbath, settling themselves in for the storm. They were joined by brolgas, ibis, and our milking cows, Daisy and Pumpkin. Marlee's birdbath is the result of my remark to Marlee one weekend that maybe we should build a birdbath in the garden, so the birds wouldn't have to drink out of the swimming pool. We were constantly rescuing birds who had fallen into the swimming pool, while trying to have a drink, only to get their feathers waterlogged so they couldn't fly.

The next thing I knew, Marlee was in the bulldozer. I certainly got my birdbath, although at forty feet long and twenty feet wide it was slightly larger than I had envisaged! But despite its size, it was full to capacity this year, with standing room only.

I am always profoundly affected by the change from dry to wet season. Gone was the brown landscape with dust billowing, perpetual grittiness of dust between your teeth and in your eyes, the ever-present flies and the heat haze distorting the horizon. In their place was over-cast weather, light rain falling—a prelude to the distant storm—and animals grazing slowly, thankful to see green grass. After pulling each mouthful, their heads were held high and their eyes closed as they savoured the flavour of fresh, sweet grass.

I settled down with a cool drink in the middle of the living room and watched the storm. Soft rain continued to fall and there was the promise of more in the deep rumbling of the thunder and the lightning striking repeatedly around the valley.

I watched the last fuel truck for the season hastily departing leaving us with our wet season supply of fuel, the driver not keen to repeat his bogging of last year.

With the fuel safely in our tanks we could officially start the wet season. When the heavy rains flood the creeks we are cut off for the next five months but life is comfortable as long as we have electricity.

With the arrival of the wet each year my writing starts in earnest, and continues daily until March. The wet is also our dreaming and talking time. It is the time when we go over the past year's events and when we look into the future.

But it was not quite time to close the doors on the outside world. First there was the Christmas shopping to be done in Darwin. Franz and Marlee were also off to a Christmas party in Katherine, their first in many years.

This party coincided with an irrigation field day showcasing many of the latest developments in water management. Living in this part of the world makes you think a lot about water. Mostly about the abundance of it during the wet season and the amazing amount the rivers generate, only for it to flow away out to sea.

257

I flew to Sydney after our Christmas shopping and Marlee drove home.

I had a meeting for the miniseries on the first day and, after many hours of talking, reading and discussing contracts, I was at the stage of being an expert on contracts. Well . . . let's say miniseries contracts, anyway. I left the meeting not sure if we had progressed or not!

Then it was time for my first premiere, *Oscar & Lucinda*! I had a wonderful night and caught up with some old friends. The party after was at Victoria Barracks and that brought back old memories.

The next night it was onto James's birthday. I couldn't remember when I had had two such enjoyable nights in a row and decided I had to do it more often. It was time in my life to stop and smell the roses.

But for the moment this enjoyment was just a temporary pause, because I had this book to finish, so I was back home late the next day.

I did take a break on Christmas Eve and called family and friends to wish them a wonderful Christmas. I just caught Susan as Ralph was about to take her to hospital! She had injured her toe in the garden a few days earlier and it had been causing her pain. The toe started to swell and when a red line started to show on her leg, they headed for the hospital. It was just as well as she ended staying up in hospital for five days taking the strongest of antibiotics. It was touch and go as to whether the doctor would operate but in the end he didn't have to.

Our Christmas on Bullo was a family affair—something we had not had for a while. The whole celebration was still a bit of a mystery to Ben who was now twenty months old. Of course the presents were the major attraction. He stood back and watched us open our presents. Then as his were piled high in front of him, he thought the best course of action would be to have someone open them for him. He elected me and stood in front of me with each present and repeated, 'Nana, Nana, Nana!' until the present was unwrapped and he had the gift in his hands. He would look it over, turn it around in his hands a few times and drop it on the floor. Then picking up the next present and starting all over again.

The next week passed quickly as I wrote day and night. Then what I had been wishing for most of the year was finally here, *New Year's Eve*. I had a feeling the next year had to be better than this one.

On New Year's Eve I always find myself sitting under the stars evaluating the year just finished. Although this year it looked as if it might be at Bullo on my own. Marlee had been battling a persistent flu for weeks. She had taken a course of antibiotics and was still not over the cough, so after talking again to our doctor, he wanted her to fly to Darwin for an examination. So despite the bad weather they took off for Darwin, assuring me they would be home before nightfall.

Being the usual worrier I am, I could see Marlee in hospital in Darwin and Franz and Ben unable to come home because of bad weather. I was resigned to spending New Year's Eve alone—well, just me and the dogs and a few trillion stars, when I heard the familiar sound of the plane engine. They were back! Fifteen minutes after they left they ran into a wall of weather at the Fitzmaurice River and had no choice to go anywhere but back home.

We saw the old year out with French champagne (although it was orange juice for Marlee) and cheese sandwiches. We watched a video because our television receiver wasn't working, and so engrossed were we in the action-packed movie that the new year arrived and we didn't realise until Marlee glanced at the clock at the end of the movie.

CHAPTER 16

January 1998 –
April 1998

New Year's Day was overcast and pleasantly cool. I took a break from writing knowing I would be back at it the next day and for months to come. Ben is so used to me sitting at the word processor that when his mother asks 'Where is Nana?' he replies, 'Nana, type.' Which about sums up January.

A cyclone moved over us near the end of the month and poured rain down all day and continued through the night. I couldn't stop myself from walking around the house and looking at the dry floors. It was blissful watching the rain pour down outside and not inside the homestead for the first time in twenty years!

The next morning I looked out over a very wet cattle station. I didn't need to read the rain gauge to tell me we had had a lot of rain!

After seven months we finally had a television receiving box that worked longer than one hour after it came

THE STRENGTH OF OUR DREAMS

back from the repair shop. After many trips to a Darwin repair shop, we took the receiver to a nice man in Katherine who gave us another receiver while he waited for parts to repair ours.

I was slowly catching up on what was happening in the outside world. I sat down that wet morning and turned on the news, only to see the main street of Katherine under water! As the news helicopter moved slowly along the main street showing the devastation, I saw all the familiar stores we trade with and there was our repairman's shop with flood waters lapping at the roof line! Only the business sign was sticking out of the water.

Over the weeks to come we realised our town was no longer functioning. All our mail went under with the post office, our television receiver was no more and we couldn't order our food or get emergency medicine from the pharmacy out on the mail plane. There were no office supplies, no clothing, the list just went on and on. Our main lifeline had just been severed.

But we were lucky compared with the people of Katherine who had lost everything! The way these people coped with this major disaster in the months to come was awe inspiring. The people of Katherine and those who came to help them showed pure pioneer spirit and good old-fashioned guts.

Our mail was dried out and put into little plastic bags. When I opened the bags the smell was overpowering which made me imagine the stench these people worked in to bring their town back to working order.

During the floods in Katherine we recorded 205 millimetres in one night. Marlee and Franz went up in

the chopper the next morning to check the lower paddocks on the Victoria River and found that the river
had flooded ten miles into our valley and there were
about two hundred head of cattle trapped on an island
of land in one of the paddocks. In the chopper they
mustered the stranded cattle across the flooded creek and
up the valley through the gate into dry paddocks. That
was our only trial in the flood that wreaked such havoc
on Katherine.

By this stage of the wet season it was fairly evident we
were going to get a very good amount of rain. We just
wished it didn't come as fast and furious as the Katherine
floods. This wish wasn't granted. The rain kept coming
in the form of violent storms and frightening winds.

Over the years it has been evident to me that wild
animals seem to know when nature is about to unleash
her fury. After the cyclone moved away from the valley
and the skies cleared I watched a tiny finch build her
nest in an ornamental figtree in a pot in the middle of
our living room.

We watched the nest being built, kept her company
while she laid her eggs and looked closely while the
chicks were born. While Mum was away busy finding
food for three very hungry mouths we would often
watch the chicks. Just a gentle touch of the nest and the
three little beaks would open wide waiting for food. If
Mum returned to the nest and we were peering in at
her babies she was very upset. But she soon realised we
were not going to harm her or her babies, so although

263

she didn't welcome our presence, she tolerated it with a goodly show of annoyance. Landing on the edge of the nest with the next food offering, she would ruffle her feathers, then proceed to feed the chicks, pretending we were not there.

I wondered why a wild bird would risk building her nest inside a house. My answer came the day after her babies were born. We had the most horrific storm of the season—even the new roof was vibrating. All the time through this frightening storm the mother sat safely and snuggly on her dry nest with her newborns. I think she knew this storm and many more like it were on their way, so she took the risk that we were a safer bet than braving mother nature.

After a director's meeting in Melbourne via a conference in Broome, I flew into Sydney to have another miniseries meeting. This was followed by a meeting with the Olympic Club organisers who wanted me to be the Northern Territory's representative for the club. I feel this concept is a wonderful way to get everyone involved and interested in the development of our Olympic Games. The club was formed so all Australians can participate in the Olympic Games. You receive information about the events leading up to the Games, with opportunities to meet athletes, attend events and even win tickets to the Games. It's a great idea. So I said yes, I would be honoured.

Then in the middle of all these negotiations I was asked to do a washing detergent commercial! At any other time I might have said no to a commercial. But with no cattle markets for years I said yes.

Now I had diversified into television commercials. Although I had been involved with the Breast Screen campaign, I see it as sending important messages which save lives rather than making commercials as such. But to advertise laundry detergent, that definitely is a commercial.

I was only home from Sydney for a week then it was off to Darwin to launch the Olympic Club. I met with the media and some officials from the Olympic Club and SOCOG who came up from Sydney. The club was officially announced and launched at the same time all around Australia.

Then it was back down to Melbourne. The evening after speaking to 650 for Senior Citizens' Week I had dinner with my dear friend Fairlie Yenchan. That's Fairlie who swam in the pool at Bullo with 'George' the seven-foot king brown. When Fairlie visited Bullo all those years ago it was a wild and woolly place and she was trying not to look too much like a city slicker. So after a few days of sharing the swimming pool with a snake that appeared every time she swam, she casually asked one night what was the pet snake's name!

When Fairlie discovered we didn't have a pet snake she suddenly lost the desire to go swimming! Fairlie is painting a portrait of me for the Camberwell Rotary Art Show from a photo she had taken at that time, about fifteen years ago. The photo showed me in a dressy

265

picture hat and jeans, sneakers with holes in them, and a cooking apron.

Back in those days I was cook, cleaner, school teacher, nurse, telephone receptionist, gardener, hostess and a few other things. By the time it got to the end of the day I was usually very tired, but still working flat out cooking, serving dinner and washing the dishes.

My routine was to finish the work and then take a long hot bath and collapse into bed.

Charlie, on the other hand, was usually drinking beer, eating cheese and crackers and reading some pirate novels all day. At sunset he would dress for cocktails and dinner, which, of course, I had to provide.

On the first night of Fairlie's visit I was still cooking when Charlie insisted I sit and spend the cocktail hour with our guest, as if I didn't have a care in the world and had a kitchen full of staff!

I sat down and he complained that I hadn't dressed for dinner. Seeing I still had dinner for around twenty to serve, the dishes to do, and breakfast for the next day to think about, I didn't appreciate the remark.

But never letting him get the better of me, whenever possible, I stood up and politely said, 'Excuse me.'

I returned a few minutes later with the very large picture hat on my head to which I had added a long bright pink scarf and a few plastic flowers to give it a touch of the ridiculous. But nothing else had changed. I still had on jeans, sandshoes with holes in them and an apron with the day's grime of the kitchen still in place.

I quietly sat down and started sipping my drink. Fairlie laughed uproariously and raced off to get her camera.

266

Charlie was silent. He wasn't quite sure if I was being funny, or if I was perilously close to exploding. So he didn't test the waters. He just gave me one of his I'll-leave-this-one-alone smiles.

The next day it was off to Canberra for the Order of Australia Council meeting which took up the next two days. I had finished my two-year term on the council which has been a wonderful experience and one I wouldn't have missed for the world. I had the privilege to read thousands of pages of the hard work, sacrifice, kindness and humanity of thousands of wonderful Australians.

I returned home to film the detergent commercial. This turned out to be a lot of fun. There was a crew of sixteen so we had people everywhere, but again we were lucky and they were great to work with.

This time I had a wardrobe assistant and a make-up assistant. Just like in the movies! Every time I was ready for a shot my make-up artist would rush out and check every detail of my face and hair and my wardrobe assistant would check my clothes. It was a very glamorous few days and I can't wait to see what all that make-up looks like on screen. No-one will probably recognise me!

The next big event was when the American *Today Show* came to do a story on Bullo, Marlee and me a few days after. Of course I had managed to fit in a conference in Coolum before their arrival. We had had such a long run of good media crews I thought Murphy's Law was sure to come into effect sooner or later. Because we wanted this to be a good shoot, I was sure this would be the time we didn't get a good crew. But I was wrong. The next few days were spent with four great people, two of whom, the cameraman and sound girl, were Australian. They were very full days, and our two New Yorkers went away with some amazing footage of an Outback cattle station, even down to Kelly, the presenter, patting a small crocodile, shades of *Crocodile Dundee*!

Somewhere in the midst of the travelling and filming I signed the miniseries contract. So despite my years of trying to slow my life down, the first few months of 1998 saw it soaring completely out of control. But these were all exciting developments.

As I finish this book it is only April and I have already shot a laundry detergent commercial, have been appointed the Territory's ambassador for the new Olympic Club, have signed a contract for a miniseries and in May will appear on the *Today Show* in America with a viewing audience of a mere seven million!

I have my fingers crossed that our appearance on this show will spark interest in my book and maybe I can finally get the book published in the great U.S. of A.! Then I really will be able to have a holiday—something I just can't seem to achieve at the present.

Of course life is never a constant bed of roses. We still have no market for our cattle so there is no promise of income from that part of our work. So the cattle will graze and grow while we move more heavily into tourism. I will also take a lot more speaking engagements than I intended to this year. It looks like my bringing-my-life-under-control program will have to wait!

So as I type the last words of this book, life once again is offering me unlimited opportunities with one hand, while hitting me in the face with new challenges and problems with the other. But that seems to be what life is all about ... or my life, anyway. And who said any problem or challenge is unsolvable?

Epilogue

*I*t is April and Bullo is at the end of another wet
season. The soft breeze and sunlight play games with
the crops, sending ever-changing patterns of silvery
waves rippling across the land as far as my eyes can see.
Nearby, cattle move slowly through a sea of feed, eating
contentedly.

I commit every detail of this to my memory for replay
in the hot, dry, dusty, windy, desolate months later in
the year. Months I know must be endured before the
next rains again miraculously change the land back into
a sea of green and plenty.

We have learned to expect these vast and violent
opposites from this land and it never disappoints us.

I remember when Charlie brought me here so many
years ago. He stood gazing out across a harsh, desolate
landscape of scrub trees and salt flats distorted by dancing
heatwaves.

But somehow Charlie saw potential. A vision for the future. 'One day you will see top-grade, stud cattle grazing on improved pasture for as far as the eye can see. Mark my words.' (A quote from Charles Henderson, circa 1963.)

At the time I thought he was insane and put the whole thing down to a midlife crisis.

But as my eyes wander over the landscape before me my thoughts turn to him again, 'Well, Charlie, your dream has finally come true. But I have the feeling that you too can see this picture of perfection; you have been very active in my dreams lately ... maybe saying, "Thank you"?

'Heavens to Betsy, Charlie, are you going soft on me? The job is done, *you god-damned, son-of-a-bitch, Yankee bastard*. Rest in peace, Charlie, your dream is now reality. Now it is my turn!' (A quote from Sara Henderson, 1998.)